THE MAKING OF A
CONTEMPORARY TRANSLATION

THE MAKING OF A CONTEMPORARY TRANSLATION

New International Version

edited by

KENNETH L. BARKER

Hodder & Stoughton

LONDON SYDNEY AUCKLAND TORONTO

British Library Cataloguing in Publication Data

The making of a contemporary translation: New
International Version.
1. Bible——Translating
I. Barker, Kenneth L.
220.5   BS450

ISBN 0 340 40263 6

*Copyright © 1987 by International Bible Society. First printed 1987. This
edition 1991. All rights reserved. No part of this publication may be reproduced
or transmitted in any form or by any means, electronic or mechanical, including
photocopy, recording, or any information storage and retrieval system, without
permission in writing from the publisher. Printed in Great Britain for Hodder
and Stoughton Limited, Mill Road, Dunton Green, Sevenoaks, Kent by Clays
Limited, St Ives plc. Photoset by Rowland Phototypesetting Limited, Bury St
Edmunds, Suffolk. Hodder and Stoughton Editorial Office: 47 Bedford Square,
London WC1B 3DP.*

CONTENTS

CONTENTS

CONTRIBUTORS

Kenneth L. Barker

BA, Northwestern College; ThM, Dallas Theological Seminary; PhD, The Dropsie College for Hebrew and Cognate Learning.

Senior Vice President, International Bible Society; Executive Secretary, NIV Committee on Bible Translation.

Ralph Earle

BA, Eastern Nazarene College; MA, Boston University; BD, ThD, Gordon Divinity School; DD, Eastern Nazarene College.

Emeritus Professor of New Testament, Nazarene Theological Seminary.

Burton L. Goddard

BA, UCLA; ThB, Westminster Theological Seminary; MS, Simmons College; STM, ThD, Harvard Divinity School.

Dean Emeritus, Gordon-Conwell Theological Seminary.

R. Laird Harris

BS, University of Delaware; ThB, ThM, Westminster Theological Seminary; MA, University of Pennsylvania;

PhD, The Dropsie College for Hebrew and Cognate Learning.

Emeritus Professor of Old Testament, Covenant Theological Seminary.

N. David Hill

BA, Grand Valley State College (MI).

Manager of Advertising and Communications, Zondervan Bible Publishers.

Earl S. Kalland

ThB, Bible Institute of Los Angeles; ThB, Gordon College; BD, ThD, Gordon Divinity School; DD, Conservative Baptist Theological Seminary.

Emeritus Professor of Old Testament, Conservative Baptist Theological Seminary.

Calvin D. Linton

BA, MA, George Washington University; PhD, Johns Hopkins University.

Professor Emeritus of English Literature and Dean Emeritus of College of Arts and Sciences, George Washington University.

Richard N. Longenecker

BA, Wheaton College; MA, Wheaton Graduate School; PhD, University of Edinburgh.

Ramsay Armitage Professor of New Testament and Director of Advanced Degree Studies, Wycliffe College, University of Toronto.

Edwin H. Palmer

BA, Harvard College; ThB, Westminster Theological Seminary; ThD, Free University of Amsterdam; hon. DD, Houghton College.

Formerly Executive Secretary of the NIV Committee on Bible Translation. Deceased.

John H. Stek

BA, Calvin College; BD, Calvin Theological Seminary; ThM, Westminster Theological Seminary; Drs, Free University of Amsterdam.

Associate Professor of Old Testament, Calvin Theological Seminary.

Larry L. Walker

BD, Northern Baptist Theological Seminary; MA, Wheaton College Graduate School; PhD, The Dropsie College for Hebrew and Cognate Learning.

Professor of Old Testament and Hebrew, Mid-America Baptist Theological Seminary.

Bruce K. Waltke

BA, Houghton College; ThM, ThD, Dallas Theological Seminary; PhD, Harvard University.

Professor of Old Testament, Westminster Theological Seminary.

Donald J. Wiseman

BA, King's College; MA, University of Oxford; DLitt, University of London; FBA (Fellow of the British Academy).

Emeritus Professor of Assyriology, University of London; Chairman, Tyndale House for Biblical Research, Cambridge.

Herbert M. Wolf

BA, Wheaton College; ThM, Dallas Theological Seminary; PhD, Brandeis University.

Associate Professor of Old Testament, Wheaton College Graduate School.

Ronald F. Youngblood

BA, Valparaiso University; BD, Fuller Theological Seminary; PhD, The Dropsie College for Hebrew and Cognate Learning.

Professor of Old Testament and Hebrew, Bethel Theological Seminary West.

PREFACE

This book had its beginning on 1 November 1980, when the NIV (New International Version) Committee on Bible Translation (CBT) decided to produce a memorial volume in honour of Edwin H. Palmer, who died on 16 September 1980 (see 'In Memoriam'). Palmer had served as Executive Secretary of CBT, as coordinator of all translation work on the NIV, and as the first General Editor of the *NIV Study Bible*.[1] The CBT agreed that the proposed volume should, among other things, explain certain NIV practices and renderings.

Shortly before his death, Palmer himself had written an unpublished article comparing the NIV and the KJV (King James Version). After his death, Mrs Palmer gave it to me, and I assured her that, after some necessary editing, I would include it in the volume being written in his honour (see chapter 14).

To make this work accessible to as many readers as possible, a simplified system has been used for transliterating words from the ancient biblical languages into English.

I wish to express my gratitude to all the contributors and to Hodder and Stoughton (Tim Anderson in particular) for their cooperation and help; to my secretary, Betty Hockenberry, for retyping all the manuscripts after I edited them; and to God for granting me the priceless privilege of

[1] Kenneth L. Barker, General Editor, *NIV Study Bible* (Grand Rapids: Zondervan, 1985).

serving Christ and his Church in association with so many of his choice servants.

Kenneth L. Barker
Editor

FABIAN BACHRACH

IN MEMORIAM: DR EDWIN H. PALMER, 1922–1980[1]

N. David Hill

The body of Christ throughout the world has suffered a great loss in the recent death of the Rev. Dr Edwin H. Palmer. The Christian community at large, and the Christian Reformed Church in particular, have lost both a competent scholar and a dedicated servant of Christ.

Born on 29 June 1922, Ed Palmer grew up and went to school in Quincy, Massachusetts. He graduated from Harvard College (BA) in 1944, following which he served as first lieutenant in the US Marine Corps 1943–6. In 1949 he received his ThB degree from Westminster Theological Seminary and furthered his education at the Free University of Amsterdam, receiving his doctorate (ThD) there in 1953. His accomplishments and contributions were so respected by the Christian academic community that, in 1977, Houghton College conferred on him the honorary degree of Doctor of Divinity.

Dr Palmer was a pastor, an educator, an author and a concerned citizen. He pastored Christian Reformed Churches in Spring Lake, Michigan (1953–7); Ann Arbor, Michigan (1957–60); and Grand Rapids, Michigan (1964–8). He was Instructor in Systematic Theology at Westminster Theological Seminary (1960–4). He wrote numerous articles and pamphlets and two books, *The Five Points of Calvinism* and *The Holy Spirit*. Besides being a frequent conference and convention speaker, Dr Palmer served as

National Chairman of the Board of Citizens for Educational Freedom (1964–8) and chairman of the New Jersey Right-to-Life Committee (1969–72).

Rarely has the Church been privileged to experience the gifts of God exhibited in one man as they were in Ed Palmer, whose two overriding attributes were his dedication and selflessness. He was constantly consumed by the call of God – a call he always put ahead of personal ambition. That was most evident in his selfless dedication to supervising the translation of the Bible into the recently published New International Version (NIV).

Ed served as Executive Secretary for the Committee on Bible Translation for the NIV from 1968 until his death. In 1979 he was appointed General Editor of the proposed NIV Study Bible. He was unshakably committed to his part in seeing that the body of Christ had the best translation of Scriptures available, by which the reader could know the Word of God with complete confidence and in his or her own idiom.

In every task Edwin Palmer undertook, he gave his best effort 'as unto the Lord'. His untimely death on 16 September 1980 has left those of us who knew him with many unanswered questions and unfulfilled hopes, but he left this life with a clear knowledge that he had served his Lord in total faithfulness.

Rev. Paul Zylstra aptly summed up Dr Palmer's life in his meditation at the memorial service on 19 September 1980, at the Midland Park Christian Reformed Church, Midland Park, New Jersey, when he quoted from 2 Timothy 4:7–8 (NIV): Ed had 'fought the good fight [. . .] finished the race [. . .] kept the faith. Now there is in store for [him] the crown of righteousness, which the Lord, the righteous Judge, will award to [him] on that day.' Ed now knows the joy of his reward. His contribution to the Church serves as the most fitting memorial to his life – a memorial the Church will cherish for generations to come.

NOTES

1 Copyright © 1980, Board of Publications, Christian Reformed Church in North America. Reprinted from *The Banner* (17 November 1980) with permission.

1 THE IMPORTANCE OF LITERARY STYLE IN BIBLE TRANSLATION TODAY

Calvin D. Linton

All verbal communication, oral or written, possesses two dimensions: *what* is said, and *how* it is said. The two are inseparable, and the *how* (that is, the style) is often as important as the *what*. Sometimes, indeed, more so. 'Doubtless you are the people, and wisdom will die with you!' says Job (12:2) to his platitudinous friends. By the use of a device of literary style, irony, he communicates precisely the opposite of what he literally says, giving bite to his rebuke and putting a stylistic burr under the saddles of his three complacent friends. 'Am I so short of madmen that you have to bring this fellow [David] here to carry on like this in front of me?' asks Achish (1 Sam 21:15). His question is rhetorical, interrogative in syntax but declarative in purpose.

So inextricably does literary style permeate the Bible (and all literature) that it is naive for some to ask (as I have been asked), 'Why cannot we simply have a direct translation of the original? Why do modern translations all sound so different from each other?' (Several times I have been exhorted to read Rev 22:18–19.)

Style is the means by which the body of writing (grammar, syntax, morphology, etc.) receives the breath of life, by which it is *animated*, breathed into, as the Lord breathed the breath of life into Adam 'and the man became a living being' (Gen 2:7). 'Style is the man himself,' says

19

Buffon.[1] If any book requires profound attention to style when it is translated, it surely is the Bible, for it is the self-revelation of God himself, through his own words and through those of his prophets, each of whom in turn is *animated* for the reader by his own style. We have never heard the rhetorical styles of Alexander the Great exhorting his troops, or of Cato crying 'Delenda est Carthago!' or of Peter the Hermit sending thousands to the First Crusade; but we have heard how style, as self-revelation, built a bulwark about England through Winston Churchill's wartime speeches, in which paraphrasable content was a secondary ingredient to the influence of his style. True, these instances relate primarily to oratorical, not written, style; but the principles are the same, and everyone can name offhand many instances of the power of literary style to change history and people's minds, for bad or good.

To think of 'style' (as some do) as mere adornment, frippery, like ribbons attached to a dress, is to miss the organic unity of all the elements of communication. True, a writer may develop an elaborate style to conceal the poverty of his content, producing sugar froth without nourishment. Gilbert K. Chesterton, for example, says of Tennyson (a bit captiously, I think) that he 'could not think up to the height of his own towering style'.[2] In other words, 'there is less here than meets the eye'.

The true and balanced wedding of style to content is a very difficult and delicate art, for both originator and translator. For an enduring marriage, the mates of *what* and *how* must be compatible. The style must not tinkle if the message roars, not solemnly intone if it laughs, not poetise if it is earthily blunt. Rather, the style must communicate (re-present) the emotional environment of the original, for though content informs us, feeling involves us and moves us. Some kinds of prose (simple exposition, directions for opening a package, instructions on how to fill out an income tax form, and the like) seek only to transmit facts, and any emotional response actually diminishes its effectiveness. But the Bible is literature, that kind of writing which attends to beauty, power and memorability as well as to exposition. It is like a rich chord compared to a single note.

Style is inseparable not only from sentences and gatherings of sentences but even from single words. The difference between content and feeling is expressed by the words 'denotation' (the content, or 'whatness', of a word) and 'connotation' (the mood, the 'feel', of a word). 'House' and 'home', for example, may often denote the same thing; but the emotional aura of the latter is greatly richer. Though many words in English possess synonyms, no two are identical, any more than the C major chord is identical with the C minor chord, though both communicate, essentially, the note C. We do not carelessly choose among, say, 'girl', 'damsel', 'maiden', or 'wench', for each carries its own connotation and affects the style. The KJV, for example, translates the Greek *gune* with denotative accuracy as 'woman' in John 2:4, where Jesus addresses his mother: 'Woman, what have I to do with thee?' But to our ears, this bears the wrong connotation – one of abruptness, almost of discourtesy, not implicit in the original. The NIV, to restore the correct connotation of gentle courtesy and respect, translates the passage: 'Dear woman, why do you involve me?' (This passage, incidentally, illustrates the difficulty of adapting style to the original mood when no single word in modern English perfectly reflects the feeling of the original. 'Lady' might be a possibility, but it sounds somewhat old-fashioned on the one hand, and has been tarnished by colloquial usage – 'Watch where you are going, lady!' – on the other.) To make such stylistic distinctions is not to tamper with the original, as some uninitiated allege, but to preserve the original in its wholeness.

I recently received a lengthy letter from a devout reader of the Bible who asked why there need be any modern translations of the Bible at all. Why cannot we simply put down God's exact words in English form? Why dress them up in so many different styles? (These questions remind one of the famous *mot*: 'If the King James Version was good enough for St Paul, it's good enough for me.')

Such questions, though amusingly uninformed, do actually touch on a profound consideration, one suggested by the great seventeenth-century poet and preacher John Donne, whose sermons as Dean of St Paul's (in his later life) drew throngs. Speaking of the style of the Bible, he says: 'The Holy Ghost is an eloquent author, a vehement and abundant author, but yet not luxuriant.'[3] This presumes that the Holy Spirit dictated the actual words of the text to the original writers, thereby (it is further to be presumed) investing the entire Bible with his own literary style. The style of the Bible, however, is not homogeneous. Rather, each writer has his own style, reflective of his personality, which a faithful translation must reflect in ways perceptible to the modern reader. 'When the original is beautiful,' says *The Story of the New International Version*, 'its beauty must shine through the translation; when it is stylistically ordinary, this must be apparent.'[4] The Holy Spirit, while preserving the inspired writers from any error, used the individuality of each writer as colours on his palette to paint a unified picture – or, to use another image, to weave a seamless garment.[5] Such exploitation of the differing characteristics of the original writers – their learning, personality, environment, literary style, etc. – in no way impugns the inerrancy of the original autographs. It merely means that God did not expunge all individuality from the inspired writers, using them only as automata or as 'word processors'. The written Word comes to us through the 'dust' of our earthly nature, but uniquely breathed into (animated) by God. It foreshadows and testifies to the ultimate revelation of God in his Son, when 'the Word became flesh and made his dwelling among us' (John 1:14). He, too, like the Bible, partook of our earthly condition (yet without sin, as the Bible in its original autographs is without error), possessing a human body, a certain physical appearance and manner of speech, reaching us on our level, that God's message may be wholly ours.

WHAT IS LITERARY STYLE?

The word 'style' itself comes from Latin *stylus* (more correctly, *stilus*), a tool for writing. This etymology is instructive, for before there is 'style' in the sense of 'manner', there must be matter – ideas, images, facts, feelings, values. To revert to Buffon, 'Ideas alone form the foundation of style'.[6] The ideal is a *natural* harmony between what is said and how it is said. The French novelist Flaubert insisted that there is only one perfect way (the right word, the right rhythm, the right imagery) to express every idea. Hence his anguished search, through a thousand revisions, for the ultimate felicity. Robert Louis Stevenson rewrote certain passages of *Treasure Island* sixty times, not hunting for what to say, but searching for a style which would not attract attention to itself, but would become the perfect servant of the content of his prose. (One result of a good style is that the reader never thinks to stop to thank the author for it!) To celebrate style as an end in itself is, as suggested earlier, fatal to good literature, though such an emphasis sometimes occurs and was widespread in late nineteenth-century English literature. Oscar Wilde famously declares that 'art [style] never expresses anything but itself',[7] a view leading logically to his further assertion that 'there is no such thing as a moral or an immoral book; books are well written or badly written'.[8] Schopenhauer, though not to be followed philosophically, spoke truer when he said that style is the physiognomy of the soul.

If, therefore, style is a fusion of the idea to be expressed and the individuality expressing it, it follows that, since no two individualities are identical, no two styles will be. And it further follows that no translation can be a perfect reproduction of the original style, for it is not possible to alter the original words without altering the original style. The goal, therefore, is to create (and it *is* a creative act) a style in modern English as closely reflective of the original style as possible. The translator must, among other things, strive to eradicate all characteristics of his own personal style, becoming a sounding chamber without string. At best, we probably must agree with the seventeenth-century writer James Howell when he says that a translator can do no more than reveal the 'wrong side of a Persian rug'.[9] Fortunately, the Bible is so gorgeously woven a tapestry that even the 'wrong side' is wonderful!

If a translation is faithfully to mirror the author's own style, with as few ripples in the glass as possible, the first task is to try to absorb the original writer's total message, personality, character, circumstances when writing, historical and cultural environment, and distinctive stylistic tendencies. It is like living in close contact with an individual, day after day, before writing a biography of him, as Boswell did with Johnson, being an observer and an absorber rather than a participant and a projector of oneself. Matthew Arnold, in his 'On Translating Homer', puts it well:

> The translator of Homer above all should be penetrated by a sense of four qualities of his author: that he is eminently rapid; that he is eminently plain and direct both in the evolution of his thought and in the expression of it, that is, both in his syntax and in his words; that he is eminently plain and direct in the substance of his thought, that is, in his matter and ideas; and, finally that he is noble.

Such general considerations may be likened to the first outline of a painting. After that come considerations of colours, brush technique, perspective, etc. Will the pose be statuesque or humbly rustic, elegant or crude, before a background of palaces or sheep-cotes? Elijah jeering at the priests of Baal (1 Kings 18:27) should not sound like Isaiah, nor Job like Hosea, nor Paul like John. The difference is style.

THE RELATIONSHIP OF STYLE TO THE TRANSLATOR'S PURPOSE

To this point the method of translation described is that called 'equivalence', in which 'the translator seeks to understand as fully as possible what the biblical writers had to say [. . .] and then tries to find its closest equivalent in contemporary usage'.[10] Such equivalence involves both matter and manner, content and form, and is aimed at making the reader in a later period *feel* as well as *intellectually comprehend* what the original writer felt and meant to communicate. This is essentially a *dramatic* method, requiring as it does that the character be given a three-dimensional reality, that he be animated. One does not wish to associate oneself with the immortals; but it may be said that the problem is the same that Shakespeare faced when he animated known characters from the distant past – Antony, Cleopatra, Julius Caesar, Coriolanus, etc. What sixteenth-century English words could be put into their mouths in place of the Latin (or Greek) which would make them live for the Elizabethan audience? Except that his job was somewhat easier: though the educated part of his audience had general knowledge of the original characters, that knowledge was not detailed or passionate (as is ours of the biblical characters), so that he could improvise pretty freely. The modern translator of the Bible is not at liberty to conceive of Hosea as a love-sick youth, Jeremiah as a sententious Polonius (though Eliphaz for this one would do pretty well!), or Job as an early Dale Carnegie.

It is a matter of the nicest discrimination to give contemporary validity without diminishing ancient awe and grandeur, or, contrariwise, without investing with dignity those characters originally seen as contemptible. A famous example of a failed effort to transmit to contemporary language (in this case, eighteenth-century precision and 'rocking horse' couplets) the style of an ancient book may be found in Alexander Pope's translation of Homer. As Dr Johnson says in his *Life of Pope*, the result 'is a pretty poem,

Mr Pope, but you must not call it Homer'. (That 'equivalence' *can* be successfully achieved may be seen in Robert Fitzgerald's or Richmond Lattimore's modern translations of Homer, and C. Day Lewis's of the *Aeneid*, as well as in Dorothy Sayers's *The Divine Comedy*.)

There is no doubt a place for other kinds of translations of the Bible. Those which paraphrase the original (such as Moffatt's in 1935; Goodspeed's New Testament in 1923; and Phillips's New Testament in 1958) help the non-scholarly reader to grasp basic ideas, though there is the lively hazard that the translator's own interpretations may colour the text, or even misrepresent it. Those which seek 'dramatic equivalence' through colloquial informality (like *Good News for Modern Man*) produce easy readability with some loss of dignity and literary beauty. Concordant literalism is highly useful to the scholar, particularly when interlined with the original languages. As for the NIV, we read in *The Story of the New International Version*, 'its method is an eclectic one with emphasis for the most part on a flexible use of concordance and equivalence' though those advising from the periphery in matters of style sought constantly for such qualities of dynamic equivalence as could be introduced without in any way compromising the highest fidelity to the content and form of the original.

A BACKWARD GLANCE:
STYLISTIC FEATURES OF TRANSLATIONS
FROM THE ANGLO-SAXON TO 1611

The earliest translations of the Bible into English (or, more precisely, into Anglo-Saxon, sometimes called Old English) give great attention to clothing the language with stylistic beauty. Though the narrative verse of Caedmon (flourished 657–680 – whose astonishing story, from status of elderly, illiterate farm hand to creator of exquisite religious poetry, is told by Bede in his *Ecclesiastical History*, IV, xxiv) is not intended to be a translation of the Bible, the happy compatibility of the blunt vigour and earthy figurativeness of the Anglo-Saxon and the similar features of the ancient Hebrew is apparent – even though Caedmon saw it only in the mirror of the Vulgate. By the time of the *West Saxon Gospels* (*c.*1000), the translator is clearly striving for a pleasing prose style, and succeeds so well that the result is acknowledged to bear comparison with the Authorised Version of 1611. Seven manuscripts of the *Gospels* survive, attesting to a wide use for that day. In one of them[11] a note states: 'Aelfric wrote this book in the monastery of Bath.' (About this Aelfric nothing is known. He is not to be confused with the famous scholar of that name, called 'Grammaticus', *c.*955 –*c.*1023, who wrote the *Heptateuch*, an English version of the first seven books of the Bible. This Aelfric, incidentally, did not hold with the doctrine of the immaculate conception of the Virgin Mary, nor with the doctrine of transubstantiation, and was cited by later Reformers as evidence that these views were not preached by the early Church.)

An examination of the styles of the translations of the twelfth and of the fourteenth centuries is fruitful and relevant to our topic, but the difficulties of the Old English language and the Middle English dialects make comment here unrealistic. (The intervening century, the thirteenth, the 'Anglo-Norman' period, has little or nothing to offer.) Worthy of note in the fourteenth century, however, is an interesting stylistic feature of the work of Richard Rolle of Hampole, a Yorkshire hermit, who before 1350 translated the Psalms (with a commentary) at the request of 'a worthy recluse . . . cald Marget Kyrkby'. Rolle embraced 'literalism', and his translation (from the Vulgate, of course) of Psalm 1:1b is as rough as riding a Yorkshire cob bareback (I have below represented the Middle English 'voiceless thorn' as 'th', and put a few words into modern English): 'Blisful man the which away went noght in the counsails of wicked, and in the way of synful strode noght, & in the chaire of pestilens he noght sate. Bot in the law of the lord the will of him; and in his law he sall thynke day & night.' English dialects varied widely in the fourteenth century, and Rolle's harshness was smoothed away when his Psalms were put into other dialects.

It is worth an interjection at this point to note an opposite extreme from the Yorkshire hermit's blunt crudeness, one of some 500 years later, emanating from Bethany, Virginia! There one Alexander Campbell (not to be confused with George Campbell of England, whose 1789 translation of the Gospels was popular) was convinced that only Latinate orotundity provided a proper stylistic garment for Holy Writ. In 1826 he published his version of the New Testament replete with such passages as: 'A city situate on a mountain must not be conspicuous' and 'Whosoever commits murder shall be obnoxious to the judges'! He was, however, trying to suit his style to his audience – in his case, classically educated men and women.

Only a little later than Richard Rolle, John Wycliffe (c.1328–84) totally altered the environment in which translations of the Bible were undertaken, in two ways: his insistence on the supreme authority of Scripture in all doctrinal matters; and his insistence that the parish priests (his 'poor priests'), who often knew no Latin, needed to be able to determine exactly what the Bible says and to communicate this intelligence to their parishioners. The stylistic goal, therefore, was to put Scripture into simple, plain, direct English. Actually, Wycliffe devoted himself almost entirely to the cause of the 'Lollards', as his followers were called, and it was largely owing to the efforts of his helpers (notably Nicholas of Hereford and John Purvey) that the 'Wycliffe Bible' (Early Version, 1382–4; Later Version, 1389) was produced. This was the first translation of the entire Bible into English, and its direct, noble style was influential on all future translations. The survival of about 200 manuscript copies of the Wycliffe versions testifies to their wide use in those days before the printing press.

The fifteenth century was a dark one for the English Bible, and it presents nothing of significance to our examination of the importance of style. Harsh measures by the Roman Church and persecution of the Lollards stifled efforts to present God's Word in a contemporary style. With the sixteenth century, however, the light broke through, with the first printed version of the entire Bible (1535), and the first great stylist, William Tyndale, ably assisted by Miles Coverdale, who followed Tyndale to Europe, where in Brussels Tyndale was burned at the stake on 6 October 1536, crying, 'Lord, open the King of England's eyes!'

It was Tyndale who most vividly declared the need for a 'modern' English translation: 'If God spare my life, ere many years I will cause the boy that driveth the plough shall know more scripture than thou dost.' (The 'thou' refers to 'abbots, deans, archdeacons, and divers doctors', to use Foxe's phrase, whom Tyndale encountered in his debates with high ecclesiastical authorities.)

The complex but fascinating story of Bible translations and their styles during the busy sixteenth century, complicated by Henry VIII's dissolution of the Roman Church of England and by wild pendulum swings between official favour towards and official prohibition of English translation, is not a relevant part of this writing. It is a fact, however, that Tyndale and Coverdale had an immense and lasting impact on the style of the Bible (particularly in the Psalms, in Coverdale's case) down through the Authorised Version to our day. Tyndale's determination to make the Scriptures clear to the untutored – even to the plough-boy – was joined to an equal determination to make them stylistically appealing. Perhaps a remark by S. L. Greenslade touches most closely the reason for Tyndale's success: 'Scripture made him happy, and there is something swift and gay in his rhythm which conveys his happiness. In narrative he has had no superior.'[12]

The immediately succeeding English translations added little to stylistic features, being largely adaptations – 'Matthew's' Bible (1537) and the Great Bible (1539). The Geneva Bible (1560), however, the first Bible in English to be printed in Roman type (not black letter), the first to use verse divisions, and the first in handy quarto size, contributed certain stylistic felicities and was mined by the translators of the Authorised Version. (This is the 'breeches' Bible, owing to its translation of Gen 3:7: 'They sewed fig leaves together and made themselves breeches.') It was the Bible of Shakespeare, and for a generation after the Authorised Version of 1611 retained its first place in the hands of Englishmen. It is a solidly scholarly work, done by learned Puritan divines fleeing to Geneva from the persecutions of Bloody Mary. They used the best Hebrew and Greek sources. The Geneva Bible caused some distress among high church and political officials, including Queen Elizabeth and her successor, James I, because of its controversial headnotes and marginal comments. (Its comment on Num 23:8, where Balaam asks Balak, 'How shall I curse whom God hath not cursed?' is 'The Pope shall tell thee.') It was not allowed to be used in English churches. For that purpose, the Bishops' Bible (1568) was prepared, a great folio. Under the direction of Archbishop Parker, of Canterbury, the task was divided and delegated, mostly to bishops with instructions 'to make no bitter notes upon any text or yet to set down any determination in places of controversy'. 'Offensive words' were to be altered, and certain passages should be marked so that 'the reader may eschew them in his public reading'. The New Testament of the Bishops' Bible, published separately, bore portraits of Queen Elizabeth, the Earl of Leicester and Lord Burghley, adding, as it were, worldly to heavenly authentication.

In style, it offers few distinctive features, but rather makes excellent use of the best earlier translations. The Psalms are carried over almost intact from the Great Bible, which was heavily dependent on Coverdale's exquisite style. In many places, the Authorised Version relies more on the Geneva than on either the Great or the Bishops' Bibles. For example, Isaiah 53:11:

Great Bible: With travail and labour of his soul shall he obtain fruit, and he shall be satisfied.

Bishops' Bible: Of the travail and labour of his soul shall he see
    the fruit and be satisfied.
Geneva Bible: He shall see the travail of his soul, and shall be
    satisfied.
Authorised Version: He shall see of the travail of his soul, and
    shall be satisfied.

It was not concern for literary style but controversy over
doctrine which spawned so many translations in the sixteenth and early seventeenth centuries – many of which we
shall not mention, as not being stylistically notable. A basic
issue of the day was whether a knowledge of the Scripture
was necessary for salvation, the Romanists maintaining
that the Church was adequate for all spiritual instruction.
Even the 'liberal' wing of the Church of Rome, as famously
expressed by Sir Thomas More, was restrictive: '. . . I never
yet heard any reason laid why it were not convenient to
have the Bible translated into the English tongue,' he writes
in the 1528 *Dialogue*; but he insists that it is requisite for the
local bishop to restrict the parts an individual might read.
Some might be permitted to read Ephesians, but not
Romans; some the synoptic Gospels, but not John, etc.
And some would-be readers – 'busy-bodies' – would be
forbidden to 'meddle' with any part of it.

It is an amazing fact (some have not hesitated to use the
term 'miraculous') that the Authorised Version, though
undertaken significantly as a practical step towards bring-
ing to some order the confusing number of translations
available, and though carried through by a committee,
turned out to be a marvel of literary beauty, the 'noblest
monument of English prose'.

When John Reynolds, President of Corpus Christi College (Oxford), recommended to James I at the Hampton
Court Conference of 1604 a new translation of the entire
Bible, the bishops present were not enthusiastic. James,
however, was. The Geneva Bible, the one then most used in
England, was infected by what he considered 'seditious'
ideas. The dividing up of the work among fifty scholars in

six groups is well known. What needs to be stressed is that among the group's objectives was the preparation not only of the most accurate translation yet achieved in English, using the most ancient documents available, but also a stylistically beautiful translation. It remains a mystery how a committee of fifty scholars (somewhat reduced by attrition as the years of labour went on) produced a unified level of prose beauty which ever since has permeated English literature like a rich dye. But some of the favourable ingredients are listed by the late Douglas Bush, the brilliant scholar in the field of seventeenth-century literature at Harvard for many years:

> [T]hough Tyndale and the Genevan group had been conspicuously learned, the Jacobean translators had at hand a richer store of oriental and classical scholarship (and fifty years later Brian Walton's learned band produced the Polyglot Bible). Then [. . .] they were working at a singularly propitious season in the history of the language and of prose style; to appreciate that fact one has only to look into modern revisions and translations. With few exceptions, the translators were not men of literary genius and do not belong to literature by virtue of their original works. But they had, so to speak, a collective ear and taste and, above all, they had intense and reverent zeal. For the Bible is the grand proof in English that in the greatest writing literary beauty is not a main object but a by-product. Of course the translators, like their predecessors, wished to render the book of books in a style worthy of its Author and His purpose, but the fundamental fact for them and their readers was the infinite importance to every individual soul of God's revelation of the way of life and salvation.[13]

Bush stresses as essential the 'collective ear and taste' of the commissioners as they sought for and retained the most felicitous renderings to be found in the Great Bible (which is to say chiefly Tyndale and Coverdale) and the Geneva Bible, always making clarity, dignity, and a pleasing verbal rhythm their major desiderata. But whatever elements combined to produce the glory of the Authorised Version, it is the translation from which no later translator can depart stylistically without some trepidation, unless correcting a clear mistranslation. The Scriptures give us warrant (Exodus 35:30–5, for example) for believing that 'inspiration' embraces beauty as well as content of God's self-revelation.

A NEARER GLANCE: FROM THE AUTHORISED VERSION TO THE MODERNS

The Authorised Version did not at once begin its triumphant progress. As a matter of fact, it was never even 'authorised'. Its literary style, which to us is uniquely beautiful, blended in with normal expectations in the seventeenth century; and despite the learning and ardour of the commissioners, their translation contains a number of errors (the first ancient Greek manuscript of the New Testament was not available in England until 1628), and its detractors charged it with 'damnable corruptions' and 'intolerable deceit', among other things. Moreover, it was slightly archaic in style the day it was published, owing to its dependence on earlier translators. This was only a minor problem, however, in a day when literary styles changed slowly, and when eminent writers deliberately employed a somewhat outdated style in order to transmit the mood of romance and beauty ideally associated with the tradition of chivalry, a tradition already dying rapidly. Edmund Spenser, for example, did so in *The Faerie Queene* (1589–96), drawing Ben Jonson's complaint that he 'writ no language'. Jonson was a kind of moderate modernist in such matters, declaring that 'words borrowed from antiquity do lend a kind of majesty to style, and are not without their delight sometimes [. . .]. But the eldest of the present, and the newest of the past language, is the best. For what was the ancient language, which some men dote upon, but the ancient custom?'[14] Bacon desired that his Latin should be

33

like silver coinage, ready in every man's pocket, rather than gold, kept in ancient coffers at home.

It is apparent that the Authorised Version generated a question which is still with us; namely, is it best to use archaic language (in our day, the discussion centres on such matters as the use of pronouns like 'thou' and 'thy', and such verb forms as 'wentest' and 'giveth') to gain 'distance' and dignity, or is it better to use contemporary words and grammatical forms to gain immediacy? Although the 'thous' and the 'thys' of the Authorised Version were entirely colloquial in 1611, producing no aura of ancient dignity, many today find 'Hallowed be *thy* name' more conducive to a mood of worship than '. . . *your* name'.

Despite the controversies surrounding it, however, the Authorised Version had, in less than a century, established itself among English readers as *the* Bible. It triumphantly survived keen-eyed scrutiny during the Commonwealth, when remnants of any royal, and particularly any Stuart, patronage came under automatic suspicion. A 1653 bill in parliament declaring that it would be advisable to make new revisions and translations, but only if supervised 'by learned persons sound in the fundamentals of the Christian religion', came to little. When this project was, four years later (and only three years before the Restoration), put in the hands of the Commissioner of the Great Seal, one Bulstrode Whitelocke, his judgment was that the King James Bible, while sometimes inaccurate, was 'the best of any translation in the world'. The Restoration naturally brought all criticism of 'James Stuart's Bible' to an end.

To touch here only on those later translations which were motivated chiefly by considerations of literary style, one may mention first Daniel Mace's 1729 version, which attempts to adapt the style to the casual, racy elegance of the eighteenth century. His rendering of 1 Corinthians 7:36, for example, runs: 'If any man thinks it would be a reflexion upon his manhood to be a stale bachelor . . .' (AV: 'But if any man think that he behaveth himself uncomely toward his virgin. . .'). In 1768 Edward Harwood published his

New Testament aimed at clothing 'the ideas of the Apostles with propriety and perspicuity', replacing the 'bald and barbarous language of the old vulgar version with the elegance of modern English'. (So much for Tyndale's blunt Anglo-Saxon simplicity, which any layman might comprehend!) Harwood completely recast Mary's *magnificat*, concluding with: 'Every future age will now conjoin in celebrating my happiness!' Peter at the transfiguration cries: 'Oh, Sir! what a delectable residence we might establish here!' (Matt 17:4). Rodolphus Dickinson, whose *A New and Correct Version of the New Testament* was published in Boston in 1833, agreed that one must get away from the 'quaint monotony and affected solemnity' and the 'frequently rude and occasionally barbarous' style of the KJV. (Samples of Dickinson's style: 'When Elizabeth heard the salutation of Mary, the embryo was joyfully agitated,' Luke 1:41; Festus to Paul: 'Multiplied research drives you to distraction,' Acts 26:24.)

Many scholarly attempts were made during the late eighteenth century and throughout the nineteenth to correct mistranslations in the AV and to incorporate the latest knowledge derived from recently discovered manuscripts, but to avoid distracting peculiarities of a purely contemporary or personal style. These do not, accordingly, concern us here. There were no significant rivals to the KJV until the Revised Version of 1885, the American Standard Version of 1901, and the Revised Standard Version of 1946, in all of which the basic literary style of the KJV is preserved. After 1961 there appeared the New English Bible, the Jerusalem Bible, the Living Bible, the Good News Bible – and, in 1978, the New International Version, Old and New Testaments. The answer to the question, 'Why, in particular, was the NIV made?' is given in *The Story of the New International Version*, previously cited, and is best read in that pamphlet.

I shall limit my concluding comments to certain specific examples of the way a scholarly, accurate, balanced translation of the Bible into modern English may be achieved with stylistic grace and with echoes and resonances from the melodic sounding board of the earlier versions. (I am competent to speak about this only from the distant periphery of the NIV, as one who had occasion from time to time to make suggestions regarding stylistic effect. If the reference be not too grim, I may say that I did but taste a little honey with the end of the rod that was in my hand. Jonathan *was* spared, you know!)

A SAMPLING OF TYPICAL PROBLEMS

From Tyndale and Coverdale to the present, the wise translator has sedulously hoarded the happiest and most beautiful phrasings, or even entire passages, from previous translators. As we have seen, King James's commissioners made this one of their stated objectives, and their product is the richest golden hoard of all. Its words, imagery and rhythms have become a part not only of our language but of our very way of thinking, and when its translation is not only accurate but contemporary, it would be folly to introduce change simply for the sake of novelty. A truly new translation like the NIV, however, must start from scratch, using the best available ancient documents and the most up-to-date scholarship, and not be intimidated by the Authorised Version peering over its shoulder.

Some passages, however, simply cry out for caution, none more perhaps than Psalm 23. Read over the centuries from countless pulpits; murmured softly to oneself for solace in the night watches; whispered in the ears of the dying; embroidered and framed on the walls of simple, pious homes; remembered on the field of battle and the raging sea – who would dare touch a single phrase! But how about 1:1b – '. . . I shall not want'? To the modern ear 'want' always means desire, not lack. So the NIV makes a change: '. . . I shall lack nothing.' And then dashes back safely to the AV.

Not everyone on the committee was entirely happy with this translation, however, and in the summer of 1983 the passage was reviewed and 'want' was restored – but this time as a *noun*: '. . . I shall not be in want.' Soundly reasoning that it is the verb form which most strongly suggests the modern meaning of 'to desire' or 'to wish for', while the noun 'want' (and also the gerund 'wanting') still denotes a lack of something needed, the translators were able at one stroke to preserve clarity and to restore the ancient sound.

And what is to be done with the AV Ecclesiastes 1:2: 'Vanity of vanities, saith the Preacher, vanity of vanities; all is vanity'? The Hebrew word, *hebel*, is used more than thirty times in Ecclesiastes alone, and suggests emptiness, worthlessness, meaninglessness, hollowness. The Latin root of our word 'vanity', however, denotes egotism, ostentation, excessive pride in one's appearance, qualities, or achievements – conceit. Thus does the modern reader understand it. So what is the best modern English word to convey Solomon's depiction of the perpetual pursuit of that which, when secured, turns out to be worthless and empty? One's mind automatically turns for help to the words great writers of a more modern period have used to similar effect. One thinks, for example, of Tennyson's 'Hollow, hollow all delight'; or of Eliot's 'The Hollow Men' (derived from Conrad's description of Kurtz in *The Heart of Darkness*). But 'Hollow, hollow, says the Preacher, utterly hollow; everything is hollow' is not the answer. Neither is 'Empty . . . everything is empty'. The NIV does as well as can be done: '"Meaningless! Meaningless!" says the Teacher. "Utterly meaningless! Everything is meaningless."' The sense is correct, the rhythm appropriate, and only nostalgia mourns the loss of 'vanity'.

And what about the AV's rendering of 1 Samuel 15:32: 'And Agag came unto him delicately'? The phrase has delighted innumerable Bible readers, including P. G. Wodehouse, who slips it into the conversation of Bertie Wooster, a young man of modest intelligence but of good education. The Hebrew, *ma'adan*, can mean something approximating 'daintily', but the context indicates the simulated nonchalance of one who is in fear of his life and is as nervous as a long-tailed cat in a room full of rocking chairs. The fears of Agag the Amalekite were well founded; for, walk he never so delicately, Samuel will forthwith kill him. The quaint word must, however, give way to the modern and accurate one, and the NIV accordingly renders the passage thus: 'Agag came to him confidently, thinking, "Surely the bitterness of death is past."' Similarly, the constant reader of the AV may cherish its rendering of Psalm 58:4–5, about the 'deaf adder that stoppeth her ear; which will not hearken to the voice of the charmers, charming never so wisely'; but 'the cobra that has stopped its ears, that will not heed the tune of the charmer, however skilful the enchanter may be', as the NIV has it, is more exact and is instantly available to the modern reader.

Such beloved phrases from the AV are not terribly numerous, and they rarely touch significantly on basic meaning; but they must be considered by the modern translator if the constant Bible reader of the AV is to be spared the momentary, diverting shock of novelty in a familiar passage, and if the new Bible reader is to be given equally undistracting access to the meaning. The danger is that in serving the latter objective, the translator will abandon considerations of style altogether, knowing that he is writing for an age, our own, which has no style of its own. Whether it be caused by the substitution of seven hours a day of television viewing for the reading of books, the 'end of the Gutenberg era' which the late Professor Marcuse rejoiced in, the substitution of 'information storage' in computers for 'knowledge storage' in the human brain, or the decline in general literacy among the students of our universities and colleges, the consequence is an era with no accepted standard of literary style, and no automatic enjoyment of an enduring style when it is present.

Happily, however, the cause of the stylistically conscious translator is not lost, for the most powerful elements of literary style seem to be innate in the human sensibility, ready to respond when stimulated and not to be totally anaesthetised even by an electronic age. The deepest and most enduring elements are those of rhythm and figurativeness, both of which mark the most ancient writings of mankind and which endure unabated today. Happily, too, these features are peculiarly susceptible of preservation in oral transmissions of culture over the centuries and are, indeed, important mnemonic devices. Such other literary devices as repetition (see Judges 5:27), parallelism, connotation, irony, hyperbole, litotes, etc., make a direct appeal in their simpler forms, needing little literary sophistication for their enjoyment. And most happily of all, it is in these basic ingredients of literary style that the ancient Hebrew is notably rich. Its vocabulary of abstract words is not large (as in the Greek of the New Testament), but it is inexhaustibly supplied with nouns and verbs, and with concrete, objective, down-to-earth (that is, nature-oriented) figures of speech, most notably including metaphors. With gratifying frequency, therefore, the translator can transmit both the literary effect and the exact meaning by means of a literal translation: 'the skin of his teeth', 'the sweat of your brow', 'the Lord is my shepherd', 'your eye is the lamp of the body', etc. (Compare this relative ease with the 'notoriously untranslatable' Shakespearean lines cited by John Livingston Lowes: 'Not poppy nor mandragora, / Nor all the drowsy syrops of the world / Shall ever medecine thee to that sweet sleep / Which thou ow'dest yesterday.'[15] Imagine putting that into German!) Even with simple, earthy images, however, it is not all clear sailing for the modern translator. Modern imagery is increasingly technological, not pastoral, and the force of the vivid metaphor used by the voice Paul heard on the road to Damascus (Acts 9:5) – 'It is hard for you to kick against the goads,' NIV; 'pricks,' AV – may not be instantly understood by those who have never driven cattle.

As to transmitting the rhythmic effect of the original Hebrew, though rhythm is more instinctively felt than imagery, the task is complex. It seems clear that the earliest poetry, including Hebrew, developed hand in hand with

music, and many of the passages we read in sober mono-
tone were originally chanted, often antiphonally and often
in very sophisticated parallel forms. (A large bibliography
on this topic exists, and no attempt can be made here to
condense even its most general dimensions.) What the
modern translator must do, therefore, is to realise (1) that
rhythm is most clearly sensed in oral renderings of the text,
not in silent reading, and (2) that any transmission of
the original rhythmic power must be conveyed through
accentual, not syllabic or quantitative metrical patterns.

Syllabic scansion is based on syllable count, with
accented syllables recurring at arithmetically regular intervals. (Such as the two-syllable iambic foot: 'BE NOT the FIRST
by WHOM the NEW is TRIED, / Nor YET the LAST to LAY the OLD
ASIDE.' Alexander Pope, *Essay on Criticism*; ten syllables,
five iambic feet per line; all neat and countable.) Quantitative scansion requires an assessment of the 'length' of a
syllable (that is, how long it takes to say it; 'hit' for example
is a 'short' syllable; 'feel' is a long one). It is a complex
system, common to Latin classical verse, but rarely
attempted in English, and then not with much success.

Accentual scansion is based on attending to the rhythm
which occurs naturally when intense feeling of any kind
animates ordered utterance. The number of accented syllables per line usually remains constant, but the total number of unaccented syllables per line is not considered, if the
effect be moving. (How the Hebrew poetic 'line' is to be
defined, in technical terms, is a matter of much debate
among prosodists.) Accentual scansion was standard in
Anglo-Saxon verse, which required four accented syllables
per line (divided in half by a pause or caesura), the half-lines
being linked by at least one alliterative sound. For example,
the first line of *Beowulf*: 'Hwaet! we GAR-DEna ( ) in GEar-
DA-gum. . . .' (Accented syllables are in capitals; alliterative sounds underlined.) Though English poetry since the
Renaissance has normally been scanned on the basis of
syllable count, much modern poetry (and particularly free
verse) is accentually scanned.

In the last analysis, what the stylist of a modern translation of the Bible needs is not only a mastery of the technicalities of prosody, but a sensitive ear, kept in tune by habitually reading aloud both poetic and prose passages, giving full value to accented syllables. It becomes quickly audible which rhythms are moving, which suit the feelings, content, circumstances of the passage, and which set the teeth on edge. The beauty of any translation is best sensed in oral rendition, and it is unfortunate that in the USA little attention seems to be given in our seminaries to teaching students to read well aloud. The situation in Britain is different. One has only to listen to the assigned undergraduate at Oxford or Cambridge read the Bible in chapel service to be struck by the contrast.

The NIV is filled with sensitive renderings of rhythms, from the exultant beat of the song of Deborah and Barak (Judges 5:1–31) to the 'dying fall' of the rhythms of the world-weary Teacher in Ecclesiastes, with myriad effects in between. As a random sample, let the reader *speak* the following lines from Job (29:2–3), being careful to give full value to the difference between stressed and unstressed syllables:

> How I long for the months gone by,
>   for the days when God watched over me,
> when his lamp shone upon my head
>   and by his light I walked through darkness!

It's better than the AV!

CONCLUDING COMMENT

Style is that which delights us every time we encounter it, without diminishment, even when the content is completely familiar to us. We do not refuse to listen over and over to music we love, simply because we know every note of it, nor do we refuse to read and re-read Shakespeare

41

simply because we already know how the plot comes out. Style, writes Kenneth Burke (he calls it 'form'), 'in literature is an arousing and fulfilment of desires. A work has form in so far as one part of it leads a reader to anticipate another part, to be gratified by the sequence.'[16] Style (or form) never sates. The body can become replete, the brain weary, but the aesthetic capability never tires. The more it is used the more it expands. Hence the importance of much reading, much study, much experiencing. Each expansion of familiarity with a work of beauty intensifies our expectations, which, being gratified, provide a re-quickened joy. The more we know, the more we enjoy what we know. If we have never read a sonnet, we do not know what to expect from this marvellously intricate art form and hence have no anticipations to be gratified. As we study the sonnet form (or any other artistic form), its world of aesthetic enjoyment opens up limitlessly. First information; then ever expanding appreciation.

And so it is with the Bible. First the *content* of God's revelation of himself and of his plan of redemption in all the Scriptures (John 5:39), made so clear by the translator that Tyndale's plough-boy may read and comprehend. Then the *form*, or style, by which the inexhaustible beauty of the Lord and his works may, even if only dimly in this life, be shown and made to be part of what we know.

NOTES

1 'Le style est l'homme même.' Georges Louis Leclerc Buffon, *Discours sur le Style* (1753).
2 *The Victorian Age*, chapter 2.
3 79th *Sermon*.
4 *The Story of the New International Version* (East Brunswick, NJ: New York International Bible Society, 1978), p. 13.

5 Ibid.
6 'Les idées seules forment le fond du style.' Buffon, *Discours*.
7 Oscar Wilde, *The Decay of Lying* (London, 1891).
8 Preface to *The Picture of Dorian Gray*.
9 *Familiar Letters*, Book II, letter 4.
10 *The Story of the New International Version*, p. 13.
11 Corp. Christ. Coll., Cambridge, 140.
12 *The Cambridge History of the Bible* (Cambridge, 1963), p. 144.
13 Douglas Bush, *English Literature in the Earlier Seventeenth Century, 1600–1660* (London: Oxford University Press, 1945), pp. 66–7.
14 'De Orationis Dignitate', *Timber: Or Discoveries Made Upon Men and Matter* (first edition, 1641).
15 John Livingston Lowes, 'The Noblest Monument of English Prose', in *Essays in Appreciation* (Boston: Houghton Mifflin, 1936).
16 'Lexicon Rhetoricae', *Counter-Statement* (New York: Harcourt, Brace, 1931). This essay is also available, in somewhat abbreviated form, in Robert W. Stallman's *Critiques and Essays in Criticism, 1920–1948* (New York: Ronald Press, 1949), pp. 234–9.

2 THE FOOTNOTING SYSTEM

Burton L. Goddard

The Bible translator's task is not done when he decides how the finished text should read. Reasons: Where manuscript evidence varies, he may judge it important to point out the wording in the Hebrew or Greek text that underlies his translation. In other cases, a note here and there will help to make the meaning of the text more intelligible. The documentation of quotations will be helpful. And alternative possibilities of translation may well be noted.

This chapter discusses the various types of footnotes and cites representative notes from the NIV.

THE OLD TESTAMENT TEXT

From early times the books of the Old Testament were copied and recopied with remarkable accuracy. They were recognised as God's word to man, and extreme care was therefore necessary to preserve them from even the slightest error. But to err is human, and in the copying process over many years it was only to be expected that some mistakes in transmission would occur.

Extant manuscripts of the Hebrew Bible have long preserved the text as it was widely known a millennium or so after Christ – the so-called Masoretic Text – and medieval manuscripts of the Samaritan Pentateuch constitute an additional independent Hebrew witness to part of the Old Testament going back several centuries before Christ. Also, several Targums, paraphrastic translations into Aramaic of portions of the Hebrew Bible, whose origins were prior to the Christian era, shed light on the Old Testament text.

Fortunately we have helpful evidence from several other sources. The discovery of the Dead Sea Scrolls, manuscripts from about the time of Christ, gives us the Hebrew text of several Old Testament books as known in the Qumran community near the Dead Sea.

Further evidence is furnished by early translations of the Hebrew Bible into non-Semitic languages, especially Greek. By the early part of the Christian era these included the Septuagint and versions produced by Aquila, Theodotion and Symmachus. Although we have only fragments of the last three translations, they are occasionally helpful in determining the original Hebrew text.

Supplementing these external witnesses to the text is the internal witness of the Scriptures. Contextual data and evidence from poetic format, particularly when in agreement with other witnesses over against the Masoretic Text, often point translators to the most likely readings of the originals.

To determine as accurately as possible the biblical wording as it came from the pens of the inspired authors, the NIV translators studied carefully all the available evidence and then decided as best they could the reading for each passage. As a basic norm, they followed the Masoretic Text, footnoting the places where they departed from it in the light of weighty evidence from other textual sources.

To understand the textual footnotes in which a semicolon occurs, one must give attention to what is on either side of the semicolon. Evidence for the reading in the NIV precedes the semicolon. If the NIV wording follows other than the Masoretic Text, after the semicolon one finds the reading of the latter, the wording generally introduced by the preceding word in the text so that the reader may easily spot where the change of wording begins:

Joshua 19:34 – Septuagint; Hebrew *west, and Judah, the Jordan,*

Sometimes capitalisation or quotation marks or a slash mark used to indicate a new poetic line render it unnecessary to include the 'pick up word':

Genesis 4:15 – Septuagint, Vulgate and Syriac; Hebrew *Very well*

If, however, the NIV follows the Masoretic Text but there is considerable evidence for another reading, it alerts the careful student of Scripture by giving the Masoretic Text reading before the semicolon and the alternative possibility following it:

1 Samuel 14:47 – Hebrew; Septuagint *he was victorious*

'Hebrew' is considered sufficient to represent the Masoretic Text unless another Hebrew witness is involved, in which case 'Masoretic Text' is spelled out:

Isaiah 7:14 – Masoretic Text; Dead Sea Scrolls *and he* or *and they*

Sometimes when one is translating back into Hebrew, one of the early translations is found not to be identical with the reading in the NIV but tends in one way or another to substantiate the NIV rendering. To indicate this, 'See' is prefaced to the notation:

1 Chronicles 25:9 – See Septuagint; Hebrew does not have *his sons and relatives.*

In some few cases the NIV emends the Hebrew text on the basis of data from other places in Scripture, judging that a scribal mistake was made. It gives the cross reference in a footnote:

1 Chronicles 6:60 – See Joshua 21:17; Hebrew does not have *Gibeon.*

Until the time of the Masoretic scholars, who laboured between the sixth and ninth centuries AD to produce the Masoretic Text, the Hebrew text was written without vowels, oral tradition supplying the vocalisation. The Masoretes did an amazingly good job, but their work was not safeguarded by divine inspiration, and the NIV translators now and then concluded that a text should be vocalised differently – their judgment determined by early textual witnesses. In such cases they deemed it unnecessary to footnote the passages. On a few occasions, however, they kept the Hebrew consonants of the Masoretic Text but altered the word grouping of the letters. In those cases, they called this fact to the attention of readers:

Proverbs 26:23 – With a different word division of the Hebrew; Masoretic Text *of silver dross*

THE NEW TESTAMENT TEXT

When the King James Version was translated, the Greek manuscripts on which the translators based their work were relatively few and not greatly different in age from our extant manuscripts of the Old Testament. But we now have many more manuscripts of the Greek New Testament, some of which date back to the early centuries of the Christian era, as well as early translations into Syriac and Latin. With these helps it is possible to construct the original text of the New Testament with a high degree of confidence.

When confronted with variant readings of the Greek New Testament manuscripts, in each case the NIV translators, weighing the manuscript and contextual evidence, decided which reading was best attested. They then translated in accordance with that reading but ordinarily without footnote record or explanation, partly because to do so would greatly encumber the translation and partly because printed texts of the Greek New Testament and companion volumes and commentaries make the textual evidence available to any who are interested. In some cases these materials weigh the possibilities and make value judgments.

However, certain types of textual notes do appear in the NIV New Testament. Two notes were regarded by the translators as so very important that they were inserted in the text rather than in footnote position. They inform the reader that certain verses which follow and which have traditionally been thought to be a part of Holy Writ were, in the judgment of the translators, not present in the original writings:

> Mark 16:9 – [The most reliable early manuscripts and other ancient witnesses do not have Mark 16:9–20.]
> John 7:53 – [The earliest and most reliable manuscripts and other ancient witnesses do not have John 7:53–8:11.]

In similar cases involving only short passages of a verse or so each, rejected words are in footnote position:

> Mark 11:25 – Some manuscripts sins. ^{26}But if you do not forgive, neither will your Father who is in heaven forgive your sins.

The most common textual notes in the New Testament merely point the reader to certain places where some or many of the Greek manuscripts do not agree with the reading chosen:

> Luke 9:54 – Some manuscripts them, even as Elijah did

Occasionally a witness not followed in the text is described in a footnote as 'early' or 'less important':

> Mark 6:14 – Some early manuscripts He was saying

A rather common footnote indicates that the text does not have full manuscript support:

Mark 3:14 – Some manuscripts do not have *designating them apostles*.

Those familiar with the science of textual criticism find the NIV textual footnotes to the point and helpful, and many lay persons learn to understand and value their witness. Other readers of the Scriptures may not appreciate fully the relevance of these footnotes, but if they have confidence in the translators as men of God wholly faithful to the inspired Word and competent in their fields of scholarship, the very presence of such notes gives added assurance that the translators were conversant with the textual data and doubtless weighed the manuscript evidence carefully.

Interestingly enough, while conservative and liberal scholars disagree on so many subjects of biblical concern, they find large agreement as to the original text of the New Testament.

THE 'OR' FOOTNOTES

The NIV translators first asked themselves about a passage: 'What was the writer saying in his language to the people of his day?' They then sought to communicate the same idea – no more and no less – through the vehicle of modern English.

Despite their expertise, they frequently found themselves far from certain about the meaning intended by the Holy Spirit, the primary author of Scripture. Grammatical, contextual, cultural, etymological, historical and other considerations sometimes did not seem to point convincingly towards the meaning and therefore to certainty of translation.

Yet after careful discussion and debate, they had to represent one of the possible meanings in the text. In such cases, when the choice was deemed important, a footnote was inserted indicating one or more alternative possibilities.

In some situations they thought the footnote reading and that of the text to be of about equal validity. In other instances the footnote represented a strong minority opinion within the translation committee. In some few cases the translators, conscious of the fact that evangelical communions not represented on the committee, and/or other competent evangelical scholars, had studied the passage diligently and come to different conclusions, felt that in all fairness there should be footnotes setting forth their views, and so decided on 'Or footnotes'. Unfortunately, there seemed to be no satisfactory way to differentiate the individual footnotes in these respects.

This being true, when the reader examines an 'Or footnote', he should not automatically say to himself, 'Apparently I am free to make a choice; in the case at hand I will follow the footnote reading in preference to that of the text.' No, at the most he should reason, 'This is a signal. Faithful translators of the Word differ at this point. The passage needs to be investigated. I will reserve judgment until I have studied it carefully. But I will keep in mind the fact that a competent body of evangelical scholars have given us the NIV text, and I will not lightly depart from it.'

A sampling of 'Or footnotes' follows:

Deuteronomy 6:4 – Or *The LORD our God is one LORD*; or *The LORD is our God, the LORD is one*; or *The LORD is our God, the LORD alone*

1 Samuel 15:9 – Or *the grown bulls*; the meaning of the Hebrew for this phrase is uncertain.

Psalm 23:4 – Or *through the darkest valley*

Daniel 9:24 – Or *Most Holy Place*; or *most holy One*

Matthew 6:27 – Or *single cubit to his height*

WORDING OF DOUBTFUL MEANING

Translators of the Hebrew Bible find their task not an easy one, partly since there is no body of ancient Hebrew literature to shed light on the vocabulary and idioms employed and partly because of faulty copying of manuscripts. Here and there the NIV footnotes inform the reader whether the difficulty pertains to just a word or to a phrase, clause, line or entire verse:

Proverbs 7:22 – The meaning of the Hebrew for this line is uncertain.

If a word occurs but once in the Old Testament, it may be especially difficult to determine the meaning:

Job 30:12 – The meaning of the Hebrew for this word is uncertain.

Notes inform the reader that we cannot be sure of the identity of many of the birds, animals, flowers, shrubs, trees and stones mentioned in the Bible:

Revelation 21:20 – The precise identification of some of these precious stones is uncertain.

A recurring note points out the fact that we cannot be sure that the body of water crossed by the Israelites fleeing before the Egyptians was what we know today as the Red Sea:

Exodus 13:18 – Hebrew *Yam Suph*; that is, Sea of Reeds.

Another repeated note warns that we cannot be sure that all the 'leprosy' references of Scripture are to be understood as the disease of leprosy:

Deuteronomy 24:8 – The Hebrew word was used for various diseases affecting the skin – not necessarily leprosy.

Through footnotes such as these, readers know at what points the meaning expressed in the text may be in doubt.

DYNAMIC EQUIVALENTS

If a point of Scripture can be satisfied better by a more general meaningful equivalent rather than the specific term used in the original text, the equivalent appears in the text and the literal wording in the footnote. For instance, the widow's 'two lepta' would be somewhat meaningless to most readers, but 'two very small copper coins' conveys the point of the remark by our Lord quite clearly:

Luke 21:2 – Greek *two lepta*

So also, the costliness of the perfume poured on Jesus's head is brought out much better to modern readers by 'more than a year's wages' rather than the literal Greek terminology:

Mark 14:5 – Greek *than three hundred denarii*

The critical reader will note that the NIV does not always put such an equivalent in the text and may or may not include it in a footnote, but let no one think that discrepancies of this kind are oversights. No, each passage was weighed carefully. The translators asked such questions as these: 'Can we be sure of the equivalent?' 'What procedure at this point would be most helpful to the reader?' 'In this passage how important is it to preserve the flavour of the text as an ancient writing, reflecting the culture of times long since past?' Each decision was made in the light of such questions.

WEIGHTS AND MEASURES

The NIV has no one pattern for expressing terms of weight or measure, but the choice in each instance was not a haphazard one. The translators tried to ascertain what procedure would be most appropriate at each point. In places one finds 'feet' (Acts 27:28) and 'miles' (Luke 24:13); in other places the reference is to 'cubits' (Rev 21:17) and 'stadia' (Rev 21:16). If modern terminology is employed, a footnote transliterates the original term; if the text has a transliteration, the present-day equivalent usually appears in a footnote.

For most Hebrew weights and measures the translators preferred to transliterate the terms, partly due to the fact that they portray better the ancient character of the writing, but perhaps even more because the traditional English system of weights and measures would result more often than not in the use of complicated fractions or decimals. Moreover, since English measurement usage is presently in a state of flux, the time may not be far away when the metric system will take over sufficiently to warrant giving first place to the metric measurements, and this could be accomplished more easily if the text could remain undisturbed.

English system equivalents in the footnotes precede the metric one:

Ezra 2:69 – That is, about 1,100 pounds (about 500 kilograms)

It will be noted that approximate figures are used for the equivalents, partly to employ round numbers and partly due to uncertainty as to exact equivalency.

PROPER NAME VARIATIONS

With some frequency the same person is referred to in the Hebrew or the Greek with different spellings of the name, and the untutored reader could easily fail to note that the individual is one and the same. The NIV, therefore, records variant spellings in the footnotes. For instance, 1 Chronicles 25:2 speaks of 'Asarelah', but in verse 14 of the same chapter, where the same person is referred to as 'Jesarelah', this footnote occurs:

1 Chronicles 25:14 – A variant of *Asarelah*

In some instances, however, the translators have regularised in the text a name variously spelled or otherwise used for a given individual, footnoting the fact:

Jeremiah 21:2 – Hebrew *Nebachadrezzar*, of which *Nebuchadnezzar* is a variant.
Romans 16:3 – Greek *Prisca*, a variant of *Priscilla*

For the most part such regularisation is limited to well-known persons or places: Jehoiachin (Jeconiah, Coniah), Peniel (Penuel), Tiglath-Pileser (Tilgath-Pilneser), Jesus's brother Joseph (Joses). Arbitrarily, to help the reader differentiate between the kings of Judah and Israel, variously referred to in the original as 'Joram' and 'Jehoram', the king of Judah is uniformly denoted as 'Jehoram' and the king of Israel as 'Joram'. In a like situation, the NIV uses 'Joash' for the king of the southern kingdom and 'Jehoash' for the ruler of the northern kingdom. Footnotes similar to those above indicate the spelling found in the original text if different from that in the NIV narrative.

Certain individuals were apparently referred to by more than one name – not just by names variously spelled. Judges 8:35 tells us that Gideon was also known as Jerub-Baal, but in other places a footnote is necessary to inform the reader of this fact:

I Samuel 12:11 – Also called *Gideon*

Similarly, footnotes call attention to the identity of 'Uzziah' and 'Azariah' and of 'Merib-Baal' and 'Mephibosheth':

2 Chronicles 26:1 – Also called *Azariah*
1 Chronicles 8:34 – Also known as *Mephibosheth*

PLAYS ON WORDS

In translating, wordplay in a language is generally difficult, if not impossible, to carry over into another language. Yet the reader loses the point unless the translator tells him what is going on in the mind of the original writer. Fortunately, footnotes can come to the rescue. A footnote is necessary if the reader is to grasp the reason why Moses was so named:

Exodus 2:10 – *Moses* sounds like the Hebrew for *draw out.*

Similarly, without explanatory footnotes, the wordplays used in Micah 1:10–15 are lost to the English reader.

EXPLANATORY NOTES

The NIV uses explanatory notes very sparingly, for a translation is not a commentary. Yet a short, judicious note here and there makes the text understandable where otherwise it might convey no clear or correct meaning. So it is that NIV footnotes alert the reader to the fact that the terms 'father' and 'son' in certain contexts are much broader in reference than he might suppose:

1 Chronicles 1:5 – *Sons* may mean *descendants* or *successors* or *nations*
1 Chronicles 1:10 – *Father* may mean *ancestor* or *predecessor* or *founder*

Likewise, footnotes indicate that the Passover sacrifice could be either a lamb or a young goat (Exod 12:3), that in the Psalms the word 'Selah' may be a musical term (Ps 3:2), that 'the River' crossed by Jacob was the Euphrates (Gen 31:21), and that the words rendered as 'fool' in Proverbs characterise one who is *morally* deficient (Prov 1:7).

CROSS REFERENCES

When a reader comes across a quotation, he wants to know the source of the quote, and since the biblical writers frequently indicate that they are using quotes, the NIV employs footnotes to document the sources of the quotations:

Hebrews 1:7 – Psalm 104:4

In a note in Exodus the cross reference points the reader to a relevant note earlier in the book:

Exodus 6:3 – See note at Exodus 3:15.

And now and then, for reasons that are obvious, the reader is directed to other Bible references.

Footnote form may at times seem puzzling. Why, for instance, do some notes end in a period while others are without terminal punctuation? The translators' policy was this: If any part of a note constitutes a complete sentence, a period will close the note. Why are some footnote words in italics? Italicised words represent either words in the text or word meanings or textual alternatives. What pattern is followed to keep the number of identical footnotes to a minimum? Ordinarily the first occurrence in a chapter is footnoted, but in most cases the note documents other similar references in the chapter. In some cases the reader is told that in a section of Scripture, as in an entire book, the same information applies.

The average reader may or may not tend to disregard the *textual* footnotes, but most readers will readily understand the other notes and find them helpful in comprehending the meaning of the text. And all careful students of the Bible will find in the notes a mine of information, giving them an appreciation of the Word they would not otherwise have. And since 'The proof of the pudding is in the eating', appropriate counsel would be: Use the footnotes. Refer to them regularly. Digest their meaning. Note how they illuminate the inspired text. Surely the reader will be amply repaid.

3 HOW THE HEBREW AND ARAMAIC OLD TESTAMENT TEXT WAS ESTABLISHED

Earl S. Kalland

The subject of this chapter may be taken in two ways. It may refer to the establishment of the Hebrew and Aramaic text itself as historically determined over the years, or it may refer to the way any group of translators, such as that for the New International Version, established the text that underlies their translation. The second of these is the main thrust of this endeavour, though, of course, all biblical textual judgment must have its source in the first activity, that is, the establishment as historically determined.

Every translator with his Old Testament in its original languages before him, and with the responsibility to translate a portion of that Old Testament into contemporary English, should have in mind the question: 'What text am I to translate?'

The Committee on Bible Translation for the New International Version produced a translators' manual as a guide for those who were to engage in the endeavour. This manual in very simple terms relating to the text of Scripture declared:

Translators shall employ the best published texts of the Hebrew and Greek with significant variants noted in the draft notes even though they may not necessarily be in the final printed product. Important text variations which are not adopted in the body of the work should be noted in the margin for consideration of higher committees.

In general the approach to textual matters should be restrained. The Masoretic O.T. text is not to be followed absolutely if a Septuagint or other reading is quite likely correct. All departures from the M.T. are to be noted by the translators in the margin.

The Preface to the NIV also speaks of the translators as 'working directly from the best available Hebrew, Aramaic and Greek texts'. Mention is made of the several editorial committees revising the translation 'with constant reference to the Hebrew, Aramaic or Greek'.

More specifically the Preface says:

For the Old Testament the standard Hebrew text, the Masoretic Text as published in the latest editions of *Biblia Hebraica*, was used throughout. The Dead Sea Scrolls contain material bearing on an earlier stage of the Hebrew text. They were consulted as were the Samaritan Pentateuch and the ancient scribal traditions relating to textual changes. Sometimes a variant Hebrew reading in the margin of the Masoretic Text was followed instead of the text itself. Such instances, being variants within the Masoretic tradition, are not specified by footnotes. In rare cases, words in the consonantal text were divided differently from the way they appear in the Masoretic Text. Footnotes indicate this. The translators also consulted the more important early versions – the Septuagint; Symmachus and Theodotion; the Vulgate; the Syriac Peshitta; the Targums; and for the Psalms the *Juxta Hebraica* of Jerome. Readings from these versions were occasionally followed where the Masoretic Text seemed doubtful and where accepted principles of textual criticism showed that one or more of these textual witnesses appeared to provide the correct reading. Such instances are footnoted. Sometimes vowel letters and vowel signs did not, in the judgment of the translators, represent the correct vowels for the original consonantal text. Accordingly some words were read with a different set of vowels. These instances are usually not indicated by footnotes.

Further specification in the Preface speaks of how the poetry of the Old Testament was handled. It says:

> Poetic passages are printed as poetry, that is, with indentation of lines and with separate stanzas. These are generally designed to reflect the structure of Hebrew poetry. This poetry is normally characterised by parallelism in balanced lines. Most of the poetry in the Bible is in the Old Testament, and scholars differ regarding the scansion of the Hebrew lines. The translators determined the stanza divisions for the most part by analysis of the subject matter. The stanzas therefore serve as poetic paragraphs.

While the NIV translators generally used the Kittel *Biblia Hebraica*, published by the Privilegierte Württembergische Bibelanstalt of Stuttgart and available in the United States through the American Bible Society, until the later edition called *Biblia Hebraica Stuttgartensia* was available, other sources within the framework of the various translators' expertise were considered. These resources are almost limitless, covering, as they do, textual references from citations of various sorts from Hebrew manuscripts, and quotations from such manuscripts and observations on such sources. The same can be said of ancient versions in other languages.

A vast amount of textual evidence is found in journals whose articles cover textual discussions. These were sometimes considered.

In regard to footnotes in the Old Testament text the Preface says: 'In the Old Testament, evidence for the reading chosen is given first and evidence for the alternative is added after a semicolon (for example: Septuagint; Hebrew *father*). In such notes the term "Hebrew" refers to the Masoretic Text.' This observation covers footnotes that relate to places where uncertainty regarding the original text occurs.

The text of *Biblia Hebraica* itself, as well as other critical texts, has its own history resulting more or less in an eclectic text. The evaluation of the critical materials in *Biblia Hebraica* was constantly in review. Other sources that the translators considered worthy of discussion were also weighed.

Some translation committees for other modern versions of the Bible published the text in the original language from which their translators made their English translation. The *New English Bible*, for instance, produced the text for their New Testament translators (*The Greek New Testament, being the Text Translated in the New English Bible*, London: Oxford University Press, 1961). A series of readings on problem passages was also published for the translators of the Old Testament (L. H. Brockington, *The Hebrew Text of the Old Testament, The Readings Adopted by the Translators of the New English Bible*: Oxford University Press; Cambridge University Press, 1973).

The Hebrew University Bible Project established an annual called *Textus* for the publication of materials relative to the determination of what the text underlying their translation would be. Material of greatly varied character was produced in *Textus* for the consideration of the translators of the New Jewish Publication Society Old Testament.

In the preface to *The Torah* (Philadelphia: Jewish Publication Society of America, 1962) it is said that their production was 'not a revision but essentially a new translation', and that 'the committee undertook faithfully to follow the traditional (Masoretic) text'. However, they found it necessary to footnote certain variants, such as: 'where the committee had to admit that it did not understand a word or a passage' or 'where an alternative rendering was possible', or 'where textual variants are to be found in some of the ancient manuscripts or versions of the Bible'.

The establishment of the Hebrew and Aramaic text underlying the New International Version Old Testament moved along with the translation process and was constantly subject to review. The structure of our procedure (and, consequently, the text) depended upon the choice of personnel and the process through which the manuscripts moved. The Committee on Bible Translation, led by Edwin

61

Palmer, selected the personnel of the initial translation committees on the basis of the expertise of such persons in the books of the Bible allocated to them for translation. These initial translation teams were to include two members who lived conveniently near to each other so that translation periods could be expedited. Two other members who served as consultants and reviewers could make their contributions through the mails. A fifth member would be an English stylist. This arrangement was not implemented in rigid fashion, but, nevertheless, remained the objective.

The manuscripts of the translations of these initial translation teams were reviewed by an intermediate editorial committee, which at first was composed of the chairmen of the translation teams. It was thought that this would facilitate the collegiate nature of our endeavour. However, the time available to the members of the translation teams necessitated the selection of additional personnel to take the place of those who could not follow the whole process.

The manuscripts reviewed by the intermediate committee were sent on to a general editorial committee composed of scholars from among specialists in theology, archaeology, homiletics, church history, church and missionary leadership, English style, etc., in order to have a broad outlook upon our task. We also sought reaction from a variety of groups as we proceeded with our work. We continued to make full and constant use of expert English stylists as consultants.

The Committee on Bible Translation itself completed the editorial procedure by considering all the details of the manuscripts produced by the foregoing committees. This final review sometimes returned to a textual judgment and translation made by an initial committee but changed by an intermediate or general committee. Then again, the CBT would sometimes concur with the intermediate or general committees against the initial team. At yet other times, the CBT would choose a translation other than that of either the initial or intermediate or general editorial committees. In this way the evidence for the text was subject to the consideration of at least four committees of scholars.

Reference has been made to the Masoretic Text and to *Biblia Hebraica* as the basic text in the original languages. Is the Hebrew and Aramaic text now available in *Biblia Hebraica* the Masoretic Text? Where did this text come from?

The Masoretic Text has a fluid history. It had its beginnings among scholars (called *sopherim* in Hebrew) in pre-Christian days, but textual materials were sparse in those days in comparison with those of early Christian and later periods. Because of the loss of their nationhood and their land in the sixth century BC the Hebrews fell back on their literary sources for continuing their identity and their character as God's people. From the time of Ezra they established certain of their 'books' as authentic Scriptures, and began the process of interpretation, transcription and publication. This is not to say that there was no copying of the 'books' that they held sacred before this time, but it is to say that attention to the Scriptures and to their study and publication (or copying) increased greatly. Before the advent of Christ the translation of these 'books' into Greek appeared, and Aramaic interpretations called Targums illuminated the Hebrew texts. The rise of Christianity gave impetus to the Jewish scribes (*sopherim*) to standardise their texts. Many variations in these texts had already appeared, as is evident from the differences between Greek, Samaritan and Hebrew manuscripts – and even more evident in the Dead Sea Scrolls.

In order to disprove the assertions of Christians, Jewish scholars such as Rabbi Akiba (*c*. AD 50–135) made notations (Masorah) in the margins of the manuscripts, so that by the middle of the first millennium AD these Masoretes had established themselves as a dominant force in textual criticism.

After another half millennium, attempts to standardise the text then current resulted in the dominance of the textual work of two families: that of ben Asher and that of ben Naphtali. The ben Asher text finally prevailed, though there are those who find ben Asher readings in ben Naphtali texts and ben Naphtali readings in ben Asher texts. Simply stated, there exists no single text that can be called *the* Masoretic Text (except as a generalisation). That is one of the reasons why critical texts like *Biblia Hebraica* exist. The editors of such texts decide what to them is the most likely reading of the original. This becomes their text. Then in margins they place the variants and the support for their text and for the variants.

Throughout textual history various classifications of variants have arisen, and reference to some of these appears in the footnotes of the NIV under the phrase 'ancient scribal traditions'. One such category is the *tiqqune sopherim*, the 'corrections of the scribes'. These usually contain anthropomorphisms objectionable to the scribes and are therefore changed to a more satisfactory reading. While there is no agreement regarding the number of these 'corrections', the Masorah generally lists eighteen passages. Nine of these are mentioned in the NIV footnotes. The *tiqqune sopherim* are known only through references in Rabbinic commentaries and Masoretic studies. The nine 'ancient scribal traditions' in the NIV footnotes are in Genesis 18:22; Judges 18:30; 1 Samuel 3:13; 2 Samuel 12:14; Job 7:20; 32:3; Jeremiah 2:11; Hosea 4:7 (two citations). This is but one of many types of variants.

It has been estimated that there are more than 1,500 variants known as Kethiv ('written') or Qere ('read'). These grew out of variations that arose because the early texts had consonants only. The Sopherim and the Masoretes after them used various signs to indicate what vowels should be added to complete the words. Several systems grew up, and differences of opinion finally produced the Kethiv (K) and Qere (Q) notations in *Biblia Hebraica* and other critical texts. Relative to this the NIV Preface says:

Sometimes vowel letters and vowel signs did not, in the judgment of the translators, represent the correct vowels for the original consonantal text. Accordingly some words were read with a different set of vowels. These instances are usually not indicated by footnotes.

Zeal for the spread of the Hebrew Scriptures led to their translation and exposition. These endeavours produced Aramaic Targums and various translations – the most important being the Greek Septuagint, which was so widely used that it was a major source of quotations in the writing of the New Testament. The history of the textual transmission of the Septuagint also had its production of variants, and these had to be evaluated by the scholars who were seeking to determine what was the text of the autographs. Early in the third century AD Origen produced a text of the Septuagint that was an attempt to standardise that version because of the many variants known in his day. Other Greek versions must also be considered.

In the footnotes to the NIV one will find indications of support for certain readings from the Samaritan Pentateuch, the Septuagint (LXX), the Syriac, the Vulgate, Theodotion, Aquila, the Dead Sea Scrolls and, of course, the Masoretic Text (MT). These sources are sometimes given more specifically as 'some', 'other', 'a few', 'most', 'many', 'very many', or even 'one' or 'two' – all suggesting variation within the source itself, that is, some Septuagint manuscripts, or a few Septuagint manuscripts, etc. Other terms, like '. . . does not have' or 'a variant of', are self-evident in meaning. They occur as aids to textual support or non-support. These footnotes introduce such variants as alternatives to the Masoretic Text that was chosen as the basic text, and they include additions to the MT and different spelling of names because of sources in different languages or because of transliterating instead of translating, or for some other such reason.

Textual footnotes may relate also to variations in numbers, or to unclear meanings though without a variant, or to a variant due to a grammatical slip, or to the substitution of a noun for a pronoun (or vice versa), or to different word divisions; or, the Septuagint especially may suggest different underlying Hebrew. There are geographical variants and those suggested by ancient scribal traditions, and plurals versus singulars. Among footnotes to the NIV Old Testament more than 400 relate in some way to the establishment of what the CBT concluded the original text to be.

These variations are due not only to the mistakes or errors of copyists. Many variants arise out of the historical process that results from the methods of written communication, such as the lack of vowels in early Hebrew manuscripts, or the difficulties engendered by differing figures of speech between languages.

One might think, then, that with all these variants, the texts from which we worked are very unreliable – but not so. The attempt to establish the original text and to standardise it was the motive behind the work on the texts throughout the history of transcription. The vast majority of variants are of no doctrinal concern. The basic teaching of the Old Testament is clear.

In a recent article Alan R. Millard presents an excellent case for careful transcription in early Old Testament times (Alan R. Millard, 'In Praise of Ancient Scribes', *Biblical Archaeologist* 45 [1982], pp. 143–53). The zeal and extreme care of ancient as well as modern scholars assure us of an authentic Old Testament in its original languages as a basis for our English translation and for translations into other languages of the nations and tribes of the world.

SUGGESTED READING

Barr, James. *Comparative Philology and the Text of the Old Testament*.
    Oxford: Clarendon Press, 1968.
Cross, Frank Moore, Jr. *The Ancient Library of Qumran and Modern*

Biblical Studies. Grand Rapids: Baker Book House, 1980 (reprint).

——, and Shemaryahu Talmon, eds. *Qumran and the History of the Biblical Text*. Cambridge, MA: Harvard University Press, 1975.

Ewert, David. *From Ancient Tablets to Modern Translations*. Grand Rapids: Zondervan, 1983.

Ginsburg, Christian D. *Introduction to the Masoretico-critical Edition of the Hebrew Bible*. With a prolegomenon by Harry M. Orlinsky. New York: KTAV, 1966.

Gordis, Robert. *The Biblical Text in the Making*. New York: KTAV, 1971.

Jellicoe, S. *The Septuagint and Modern Study*. Oxford: Clarendon, 1968.

Klein, Ralph W. *Textual Criticism of the Old Testament*. Philadelphia: Fortress Press, 1974.

McCarter, P. Kyle, Jr. *Textual Criticism: Recovering the Text of the Hebrew Bible*. Philadelphia: Fortress Press, 1986.

Roberts, B. J. *The Old Testament Text and Versions*. Cardiff: University of Wales Press, 1951.

Waltke, Bruce K. 'The Textual Criticism of the Old Testament', in *Biblical Criticism* by R. K. Harrison *et al.* Grand Rapids: Zondervan, 1978, pp. 45–82.

Würthwein, Ernst. *The Text of the Old Testament*. Translated by E. F. Rhodes. Grand Rapids: Eerdmans, 1979.

4 THE RATIONALE FOR AN ECLECTIC NEW TESTAMENT TEXT

Ralph Earle

What Greek text was used by the translators of the NIV New Testament? It was basically that found in the United Bible Societies' and Nestle's printed Greek New Testaments, which contain the latest and best Greek text available.

In many passages there is no way of being absolutely certain as to what was the original reading because the best Greek manuscripts, both earlier and later ones, have variant readings. In such cases the translators were asked to weigh the evidence carefully and make their own decision. Of course, such decisions were subject to re-examination by the Committee on Bible Translation. In the UBS text the adopted readings are marked with an A, B, C, or D. Those marked 'A' are virtually certain, 'B' less certain, 'C' doubtful, and 'D' highly doubtful. It is the last, especially, that have to be weighed carefully.

All the Greek manuscripts are written by hand. This is the meaning of 'manuscript' – from the Latin *manu*, 'by hand', and *scriptus*, 'written'. It would be almost impossible for a scribe to copy the entire Greek New Testament without making any mistakes. This is especially true in the older Greek manuscripts, which have not only no chapter and verse divisions and no separation into sentences (no punctuation marks), but not even any separation between words. All we have are thousands of consecutive Greek letters in line after line, column after column, page after page, through a whole book of the New Testament. This made the task of copying exceedingly difficult. Even typists today will sometimes skip a line if two consecutive lines begin or end with the same word. This same error, as would be expected, is found in ancient Greek manuscripts. Fortunately, we now have a little over 5,000 Greek manuscripts of the New Testament, in whole or in part. By careful comparison of these we can weed out most errors made in copying.

For the past 300 years the most widely used English translation of the Bible was the King James Version (1611). The New Testament of this was based on the so-called Textus Receptus ('Received Text'), which is essentially the same as the Majority Text and the Byzantine text-type. Since some people are still defending the superiority, and even the infallibility, of the TR, it might be well for us to look at its origin and nature.

The first published printed Greek New Testament was made by Erasmus, the famous Dutch scholar. At the urging of a publisher who wanted to make a 'scoop', he prepared it very hastily, as he himself admitted. He had only about half a dozen Greek manuscripts, none of them earlier than the tenth century AD. Now we have two dozen manuscripts from the third century, a dozen from the fourth century, and about 200 from the fifth to ninth centuries that have already been examined carefully. Certainly the Greek text we use today is far more reliable than that produced by Erasmus in his third edition of 1522. It was this edition, as very slightly modified by Stephanus and Elzevir, that became known as the Textus Receptus used by the King James translators. It is a text based primarily on late medieval manuscripts, which were the result of copying and re-copying across the centuries.

The oldest manuscripts were written on papyrus, from which we get our word 'paper'. It was made by taking strips from the papyrus plant – which one can still see growing near the banks of the Nile river in Egypt and in shallow water in northern Galilee. These strips were laid side by side vertically. Then horizontal lines of strips were laid across them, and the two layers were glued together. Writing was done primarily on the horizontal strips, though sometimes the back of the page was used.

Apparently the books of the New Testament were written on papyrus for the first three centuries. Since this material was so fragile, most of the papyrus manuscripts of New Testament books perished long ago. But in the dry sands of southern Egypt some of these have been found during the last fifty years (beginning in the 1930s). As noted above, we now have about twenty-five Greek New Testament papyri from the third century.

It has been said that there is not known to exist today any copies of the Greek classical authors' writings from within 800 years of their composition. But we now possess two copies of John's Gospel (Papyri 66 and 75) from about AD 200 – close to 100 years from the time the Gospel was written (*c.* AD 95). This is a spectacular gain!

In the fourth century the shift was made pretty much from papyrus to vellum (skins of young animals). The New Testament manuscripts from the fourth to ninth centuries are called 'uncials' – literally 'inch-high', because written in large, square capital letters. Manuscripts from the ninth to fifteenth centuries are called 'minuscules', because written in small letters. They are also known as 'cursives' (running), because they are written in a running script. We have about 2,400 cursive New Testament manuscripts, as against about 270 uncials.

In 1859 Constantin Tischendorf discovered in the monastery of St Catherine on Mount Sinai a fourth-century uncial manuscript of the entire New Testament, together with much of the Old Testament in Greek translation. From its place of discovery it is called Codex Sinaiticus. ('Codex' means a bound book, as distinct from a scroll.) Soon after that, he pressured authorities into making another fourth-century manuscript available to scholars. It is called Codex Vaticanus, because held in the Vatican Library at Rome. Codex Sinaiticus is now in the British Museum.

These two great fourth-century uncials agree rather closely with the third-century papyri. This provides us with a more accurate Greek text of the New Testament than that found in the Textus Receptus, which is based primarily on late minuscules. We should be grateful to God for making these early manuscripts available to us as the basis for an up-to-date, contemporary translation based on an ancient text.

The importance of making a careful examination of manuscript evidence may be illustrated by checking the footnotes that deal with textual differences (in the New Testament). We want now to look at a few of these.

The first one is on Matthew 5:22. Footnotes are indicated in the text of the NIV by small letters (in alphabetical order). The footnote carries this letter, followed by the verse number. Then one finds in italics the last word before the raised letter in the text, followed by the addition or change indicated. Here we find that 'Some manuscripts' add 'without cause' (cf. KJV). But the additional Greek *eike* is not in the earliest manuscript (Papyrus 67, *c*. AD 200), nor in the two fourth-century manuscripts. It is understandable how a later scribe might add this modifier to soften the rigour of this warning.

The second textual footnote is on Matthew 5:44. Here it is 'Some late manuscripts' that add: 'bless those who curse you, do good to those who hate you' (cf. KJV). Here the evidence is even stronger against the addition.

More important is the doxology at the end of the Lord's Prayer (Matt 6:13) 'for yours is the kingdom and the power and the glory for ever. Amen.' With the exception of W (fifth century) this is not found in any manuscript earlier than the ninth century. It is easy to see how it would be added by someone as a fitting closing of the prayer, but it is very clear that it was not a part of the original text of this Gospel.

In the NIV, Matthew 17:21 (KJV) is entirely missing. Why? To answer that question, we should first turn to Mark 9:29. There Jesus is reported as saying to his disciples: 'This kind can come forth by nothing, but by prayer and fasting' (KJV). We once heard a godly missionary say, 'If you don't get the answer to your prayer, then fast and God will have to answer your petition.' But that is magic – manipulating God – not true religion. The fact is that 'and fasting' is not found in our two fourth-century manuscripts (cf. NIV). It apparently was added in the fifth century, when much emphasis was being given to Gnostic asceticism and to monasticism. Then the whole of Mark 9:29 was inserted in Matthew. But Matthew 17:21 is not found in our two earliest manuscripts, as well as in the best ninth-century codex. At best, it is very doubtful if these words are genuine, and so they should not be emphasised.

The most notorious case of an added reading (in the TR) – and in this case there is no doubt about its having been added – is found in 1 John 5:7. It is the strongest statement in the KJV on the Trinity, but it has no basis in the Greek text. It is found in the KJV, of course, because it is in the Textus Receptus. How did it get there? Erasmus did not have it in his first edition of the Greek New Testament (1516) or his second edition (1519). It is thought that because of Roman Catholic pressure – since the passage was in the Latin Vulgate – Erasmus put it in his third edition (1522). Martin Luther wisely did not include it in his German New Testament of that same year. It seems that Roman Catholics produced Codex Montfortianus, inserting this passage from the Latin. We have personally examined this sixteenth-century manuscript in Dublin. The passage is found in the text of only one other manuscript (fifteenth-century).

The facts are that these added words are not quoted by any Greek fathers of the early Church and are absent from all the early versions. They were not in the text of the original Latin Vulgate made by Jerome, but were inserted later. There can be no doubt today that the words are not a part of the original text of 1 John.

All these facts that we have been rehearsing may seem rather disconcerting to the average reader. But, as we noted before, with thousands of Greek manuscripts of the New Testament now at our disposal, we can reach a high degree of certainty with regard to the probability of the best text. It should be added that comparative statistical studies indicate that all Greek manuscripts are in essential agreement on at least 95 per cent of the New Testament text. Significant differences exist, then, in less than 5 per cent of the total text. And it must be said emphatically that none of these variant readings poses any problem as to the basic doctrines of the Bible. They are intact! We should like to add that all the members of the Committee on Bible Translation are devout evangelicals, believing in the infallibility of the Bible as God's Word. We have all sought earnestly to represent as accurately as possible what seems to be, as nearly as we can determine, the original text of the New Testament.

SUGGESTED READING

Brown, Kenneth I. *A Critical Evaluation of the Text of the King James Bible*. Allen Park, MI: Detroit Baptist Divinity School, 1975.

Carson, D. A. *The King James Version Debate*. Grand Rapids: Baker Book House, 1979.

Ewert, David. *From Ancient Tablets to Modern Translations*. Grand Rapids: Zondervan, 1983

Fee, Gordon D. 'The Textual Criticism of the New Testament', in *Biblical Criticism* by R. K. Harrison *et al*. Grand Rapids: Zondervan, 1978, pp. 125–55.

Greenlee, J. Harold. *Introduction to New Testament Textual Criticism*. Grand Rapids: William B. Eerdmans, 1964.

Lewis, Jack P. *The English Bible from KJV to NIV*. Grand Rapids: Baker Book House, 1982.

MacRae, Allan A., and Robert C. Newman. *The Textus Receptus and the King James Version*. Hatfield, PA: Biblical Theological Seminary, 1975.

Metzger, Bruce M. *The Text of the New Testament*. New York: Oxford University Press, 1968.

—— *A Textual Commentary on the Greek New Testament*. New York: United Bible Societies, 1975.

Sheehan, Bob. *Which Version Now?* Sussex, England: Carey Publications, n.d.

5 WHY HEBREW *SHE'OL* WAS TRANSLATED 'GRAVE'

R. Laird Harris

The translation of the Hebrew word *she'ol* (popularly written Sheol) is an old problem. Its translation brings up a number of theological as well as linguistic matters. It occurs sixty-five times in the Old Testament. Thirty-one times the KJV rendered it 'grave'; most of the other occurrences were rendered 'hell'. Numbers 16:30,33 and Job 17:16 are the exceptions. Obviously the word refers to some aspect of death, but there is discussion as to exactly what it means. There is also discussion as to what the word can refer to – what is the situation of a person at death? And further, what did the people of the Old Testament know about the situation of a person at death?

In the face of these theological differences, a number of modern versions simply do not translate the word *she'ol*. They transliterate it as Sheol, usually capitalised, and leave each reader to decide for himself what the Hebrew word means. The NIV translators studied the matter and came to a decision as to the meaning of the word. It is our purpose to summarise that study with a view to justifying the decision. It should be emphasised, however, that the NIV does put a footnote ('Hebrew *Sheol*') at every place where the word is used so that in any case the English reader will have the data and can judge the translation for himself.

In studying the word Sheol, little help comes from outside the Bible. The word was not used outside the Jewish

75

community or in other Semitic languages except in Jewish Aramaic. It does occur once in the Jewish Aramaic from Elephantine of about 400 BC.[1] The case is not clear, but the meaning 'grave' fits. The only other extra-biblical usage is on the lid of an ossuary found in Jerusalem. These ossuaries were little stone boxes into which the bones of the departed were gathered some time after burial and decay. The lid of the box has the word 'Sheol' scratched on it. The meaning 'grave' would seem to fit as the box was the resting place of the remains of the person.

Before turning to the biblical passages the various theories should be listed so that it will be apparent what we have to choose from. One theory is that Sheol refers to the place of departed spirits. Other ancient cultures pictured the dead spirits as going to a cheerless underworld to live a meagre and shadowy existence, where they ate clay and were generally deprived of light and happiness. The Akkadians did not picture them as being in penal suffering. The Egyptians pictured the experience of death as a ship's voyage through many hazards to arrive at last (if lucky) at a land of happiness.

The Bible has none of these rather weird views. But it does present what is a difficulty to the New Testament believer: both wicked (Num 16:3) and righteous (Gen 38:35) go to Sheol. A view was therefore early developed that said that there were two compartments in Sheol, an upper part for the believers and a lower for the lost. The upper part was not too well defined – it was the *limbus patrum*, where the fathers were held in limbo until Christ died. At that time Christ went down to Sheol. The evidence for this is cited as 1 Peter 3:18–20, with corroboration from 1 Peter 4:6 and Ephesians 4:9. In Sheol Christ announced his salvation to the unbelievers (without results) and also to the believers, who were released and taken into heaven, where they are now. The growing belief may have had some connection with the phrase in the Apostles' Creed, 'He descended into hell,' which first appears about AD 400 in the Latin Creeds: *descendit ad inferos*.

This view has some problems. It seems to be built up just to accommodate the word Sheol. Its biblical and theological bases are poor. Surely Ephesians 4:9 has no bearing on the subject. The NIV translation is well supported. Christ who ascended from earth to heaven is the same Jesus who came down from heaven to the earth below in his incarnation. It says nothing about a descent into hell. Also 1 Peter 4:6 certainly refers to a preaching in olden time to people who lived then but are now dead. It does not say that the gospel was preached to them after they died.

Even 1 Peter 3:18–20 cannot be said to prove this view: it says that Christ preached through the Spirit to the spirits in prison who disobeyed long ago. The apostate days of Noah were the times of these wicked men. The verse does not at all say that Christ descended and personally announced the cross to these people. These people, while they were alive, heard the message. It was the message preached by the Spirit of Christ through Noah. They rejected it and are now in their eternal prison. To hang any teaching about Sheol on this verse would be tenuous indeed. We have other evidence that Christ, when he died, went straight to heaven (Luke 23:43). And Christ, in his illustration of the rich man and Lazarus, specifically tells of a great gulf between Abraham's bosom, where Lazarus was (before the cross!), and hell, where the rich man was (in conscious torment).

There are others who say that the Old Testament teaches soul sleep. The New Testament seems clearly to contradict this. We have cited the story of the rich man and Lazarus in Luke 16. Paul is equally clear in 2 Corinthians 5:8. John was given a glimpse of heaven and saw multitudes of the redeemed there (Rev 7:9). Some of the redeemed had suffered a martyr's death and were told to wait awhile until others should follow in their steps (Rev 6:11). But does the Old Testament teach soul sleep? Much depends on one's interpretation of Sheol. If Sheol is the habitation or condition of spirits and if it is a place of darkness, forgetfulness and oblivion (cf. Ps 88:10–12), then there is some argument for the sleep of the soul of both the righteous and the wicked until the judgment day or at least until the cross. On the other hand, if the darkness, oblivion and forgetfulness of Sheol refer only to the body in the grave, then these verses say nothing at all about soul sleep or about the distinction or lack of distinction between the saved and the lost. Since soul sleep is clearly negated by the New Testament (even before the cross), and since the Old Testament itself (as we shall see) indicates that believers enjoy the presence of God, it seems best to question this particular view of Sheol that is said to fit the soul sleep theory. After all, the Old Testament nowhere says that Sheol is the place of departed spirits. The KJV translators, at least, thought that many of the Old Testament passages referred to the place of dead bodies – the grave.

There are a number of places where the translation 'grave' is natural if not preferable. In these places the KJV has used the word 'grave' (Gen 37:35; 42:38; 44:29; cf. 44:22). Probably the same usage applies to the deaths of Joab and Shimei in 1 Kings 2:6,9. Solomon was surely not capable of sending Shimei to hell, but he had him and Joab killed with dispatch. In the fulfilment of David's last command to Solomon it simply says that Benaiah killed Joab and Shimei (1 Kings 2:34,46). To bring Shimei's grey hairs down to Sheol in blood (2:9) surely refers only to his death, not to the condition of his soul after death or to any punishment beyond his execution. Joab was in rebellion against Solomon. We have no information that Joab was unfaithful to God or that he went to hell at his death. He died at the altar, where he had fled.

There are some more debatable passages, among them the case of Korah and his company (Num 16:30,33). The KJV says that Dathan and Abiram and their possessions went down 'quick into hell'. The word 'quick' used here, of course, does not mean 'suddenly'. It is the Old English usage of 'quick' meaning 'alive'. We would say that they were buried alive: 'They went down alive into the grave.' Their tents and other possessions obviously did not go to a place of departed spirits or into hell. These rebels may indeed have gone to hell. But the text does not go that far. It merely says they died in this miraculous way. Regarding further punishment after their death, the text is silent. Psalm 55:15 is quite similar and probably means no more.

Other passages in the historical books are few. These few are mostly found in poetical passages. And there may be a reason. It has been suggested that Sheol is a poetical synonym for *qeber* ('the grave'). We shall see a number of places where these two words are used as synonyms in poetry.

In 1 Samuel 2:6, Hannah praises the Lord as one who 'brings down to Sheol and raises up'. The parallel line says he 'brings death and makes alive'. It may be argued whether she was speaking of death and resurrection or of preservation from death. Surely she did not speak of consignment to hell and release therefrom. Possibly she was speaking of going to some underworld of spirits and coming back. But the parallel line gives no hint of this. It only says, 'He brings death and makes alive.'

It may be of some significance that in 1 Samuel 28:11–19 there is no mention of Sheol. The witch 'brought up' Samuel. Samuel apparently knew of the impending battle and the continuing popularity of David. He adds the significant item, 'Tomorrow you and your sons will be with me.' We remember David's later words concerning his child, 'I will go to him, but he will not return to me' (2 Sam 12:23). Sheol is not mentioned here, but soul sleep hardly fits either. We may compare the souls under the altar in Revelation 6:11, who were told to 'wait a little longer' (NIV 'rest a little longer', Greek *anapausontai*), but they were fully conscious. The text does not imply that Samuel was sleeping. He was just brought back temporarily to a world of trouble and woe.

Many times the word Sheol is parallel to or in close context with other words for death and burial. These contexts give a good idea of the meaning of the word. Notable are the passages in Ezekiel. The word is used five times in

Ezekiel 31 and 32 and nowhere else in the book. The passage is the lament for Pharaoh with the prophecy of his demise. Pharaoh is compared to Assyria in its power and pride. It is not clear whether the description of Assyria is very short or whether it runs to 31:17. For our purpose it does not matter. All the nations mentioned in the passage are destined for 'death' (*mawet*), for the 'earth below' (*'eres taḥtit*) with those who go down to the 'pit' (*bor*). Then it says, twice, that God brought it (Assyria or Egypt) down to the 'grave' (Sheol, vv. 15–16) with those who go down to the 'pit'. The other nations, the 'trees of Eden', were consoled in the 'earth below'. The allies had also gone down to the 'grave' (Sheol), joining those killed with the sword (vv. 16–17). The description repeats a good bit. Presumably all these terms are synonymous.

Chapter 32 is much the same with more repetition. Babylon will conquer Egypt (vv. 11–12). The hordes of Egypt will be consigned to the 'earth below' with those who go down to the 'pit'. There from within the 'grave' (Sheol) they welcome Egypt who now lies 'with the uncircumcised, with those killed by the sword' (vv. 18–21). The following paragraphs mention Assyria, Elam, Meshech, Tubal, Edom and the Sidonians, saying similar things of each. Assyria is there surrounded by the 'graves' (*qeber*) of her slain in the 'depths (or sides) of the pit' (vv. 22–3). Elam is in her 'grave' (*qeber*) with her hordes who went down uncircumcised to the 'earth below' with those who go down to the 'pit', with her hordes around her 'grave' (*qeber*, vv. 24–5). Meshech and Tubal have their hordes around their 'graves' (*qeber*). They lie with the others who, uncircumcised, went down to the 'grave' (Sheol) 'with their weapons of war, whose swords were placed under their heads' (vv. 26–7). Edom and the Sidonians also lie with the uncircumcised who go down to the 'pit' (vv. 29–30).

The excessive repetition of these verses seems to make it mandatory that the terms are synonymous. There are figures of speech, of course. But the figures are the figures of death and burial. The nations lie slain. Their weapons are with them – their swords under their heads. Six times the word *qeber* is used, which never elsewhere refers to anything but a grave. The word *bor* ('pit') is also quite appropriate for grave. A *bor* was dug. Ancient graves of the Israelite period were caves dug with flat bench-like niches cut at the sides of the tomb, on which new bodies were laid when the old ones had decayed into dust. The phrase 'earth below' says nothing about a large cavern below the earth. It is quite applicable to the usual tomb dug below ground, often with a vertical shaft, at the bottom of which was a stone covering the entrance to the hollowed-out cave. There the bodies were laid with pottery and sometimes weapons. 'Grave' (*qeber*) is paralleled in v. 24 with the 'earth below'. The grave was a place of darkness and decay.

A similar mixing of terms is found in Psalm 88. The word Sheol is used in v. 3, 'pit' in vv. 4,6 (the 'lowest pit' or the 'pit below'). The place is called a grave (*qeber*) in vv. 5,11. The dead are called *metim* in vv. 5,10. The parallel to this word in v. 10 is *rᵉpha'im* (often translated 'shade' because of its assumed etymology, but never used to mean more than 'dead ones'). In v. 11, the word 'grave' (*qeber*) is paralleled with Abaddon ('destruction'), and the grave/Abaddon is called a place of darkness and oblivion in v. 12. Of these people in the tomb (*qeber*) the text asks in v. 10, 'Do those who are dead rise up and praise you?' This lack of praise characterises the tomb, not some fancied underworld. It does not teach soul sleep but only refers to the stillness of the body when 'this cold stammering tongue lies silent in the grave', as the hymn has it.

The same thing is said of Sheol in Psalm 6:5, where Sheol is paralleled with death. The curse on the wicked is that they might lie silent in the 'grave' (Sheol) (Ps 31:17), which may only be a wish for their sudden death. In Psalm 30:9, in connection with the 'pit' (*shaḥat*), the question is: 'Will the dust praise you?' – a question most appropriate for the dust and decay of the body in the tomb. This verse is explained somewhat by v. 3, which says, 'you brought me up from the grave (Sheol); you spared me from going down to the pit (bor).' The terms bor and shahat are used similarly to Sheol. The psalmist thanks God that he was spared from death, the pit, the dust, the decay, where his dust will lie in silence and not take part in the worship of God. If Sheol here refers to departed spirits, it proves too much! It would prove soul sleep at the least. Much better to find in these terms only a reference to the body and its decay.

Some attention must be given to this term shahat, often translated 'pit'. It is said to come from the verb shuah ('dig') and indeed is used of a pit dug for a lion trap (Ezek 19:4,8), or for a snare in general (Pss 7:15; 9:15; 35:7), or for the dungeon of a prison (Isa 51:14). However, the word is also used numbers of times in some relation to the grave. This can be the same word, inasmuch as the grave was a cavern dug in the earth. On the other hand, there could be a second word shahat derived from the verb shahat ('to corrupt, destroy'). A similar double noun or pair of nouns (nahat), meaning both 'rest' and 'descent', from the roots nuah and nahat – the one meaning 'to rest' and the other 'to go down' – may be cited for illustration. In any case, the noun shahat seems clearly to mean 'corruption' in Job 9:31; 17:14. In Isaiah 38:17 there occurs the expression 'pit of destruction' (shahat b^{e}li), which has both Sheol and bor ('pit') in close association (v. 18). It apparently refers to the grave as a place of decay.

There is a picture somewhat similar to Isaiah 38:17 in Psalm 49:9–14. The words qeber, 'grave' (v. 11, LXX text), Sheol (v. 14 – lines a, d – and v. 15) and shahat ('pit') are used in the passage. Though the Hebrew word for 'form' (v. 14 d, NIV) is somewhat uncertain, still v. 14 d speaks of decay in the grave (Sheol). This whole section of the psalm contrasts the perishing of the wicked in their death (vv. 10, 12 – LXX text – 20, etc.) with the deliverance of the righteous from the power of Sheol. God will 'take the righteous to himself' (v. 15). With this in mind, the contrast of vv. 7–9 can well be seen as the futile desire of the wicked for eternal life versus the fact of their wasting away in the grave (v. 9). To 'not see shahat' seems to be more than continuing this life here and now. It is rather to live with God and not decay or 'perish' in the grave. The problem of vv. 7–9 is similar to that of Psalm 89:48, with which there are verbal parallels. No one 'can live and not see death or save himself from the power of the grave'. In Psalm 89 the psalmist's appeal is to God's covenant with David, which surely did not include David's living on for ever in this life, nor did it include merely the continuity of his kingly line. As Dahood has argued in his commentary on the Psalms,[2] such passages affirm the hope of eternal life, whereas the wicked will not 'live on for ever and not see decay' (Ps 49:9).

These usages of *shaḥat* do not, perhaps, set the meanings of 'pit' and 'corruption' in opposition. The 'corruption' spoken of is almost always the corruption or decay of the grave, which in antiquity was certainly a pit. To 'see the pit' was to experience the decay of the grave, which has dust for its main component.

With this background, the use of Sheol in Psalm 16:10 becomes clearer. The psalmist has affirmed his integrity and his total dependence on God and his confidence in God's total care (vv. 1–8). Therefore his heart, liver (taking KJV 'glory' as *kabed*, 'liver', an organ of sensitivity and feeling, as other languages use 'heart', 'mind', or 'tongue') and flesh rest secure. The further and final reason for his joy is that God will not 'abandon him', 'give him over' to Sheol, or let his Holy One see 'decay' (*shaḥat*). With one voice most other modern translations here translate *shaḥat* as 'pit'. Some by capitalisation seem to particularise it as some underworld place. The derivation from *shaḥat* (to destroy, corrupt') is not much considered. But the meaning 'decay' is amply attested. And this meaning of the phrase 'to see corruption' may be accepted as 'experiencing corruption' even if *shaḥat* is taken as the 'tomb'. 'Not to see *shaḥat*' may well mean not to be left under the power of the grave with the consequent dissolution of the body into the dust of the grave.

It appears that this verse does not speak of mere continuation of earthly existence because of some deliverance from danger. The next verse gives the contrast, the state that the subject of the psalm will attain – in a word, heaven. The verse is quite similar to Psalm 21:6, where the question is: does this refer to David's experience in this life or to his hope of heaven? Dahood,[3] on the basis of verbal parallels with Ugaritic, argues convincingly that Psalm 21:4 refers to eternal life and holds that this verse accordingly refers to David's expectation of heaven. He naturally says the same thing of Psalm 16:11,[4] and rightly so. It is true, of course, that the believer is in the presence of God in this life. Yet even Paul could say that when 'we are at home in the body, we are away from the Lord' (2 Cor 5:7). David was happy to be at God's temple (cf. Ps 84). He would seek the Lord there (Ps 27:4). In memorable words David claims the Lord's nearness as his Shepherd (Ps 23:1), but the ultimate blessing he envisions is after life is over, 'to dwell in the house of the Lord for ever' (Ps 23:6).

Surely the most natural interpretation of Psalm 16:11 is to refer it to heaven. In this life the psalmist has God at his right hand; in that day he will be at God's right hand, for ever in his presence in perfect joy. The description is somewhat like that of the final verse of the next psalm (17:15); there again the psalmist will be satisfied with the vision of God when he 'awakes' – a word used of resurrection in Daniel 12:2 and elsewhere. The plainest interpretation of Psalm 16:10–11, therefore, is that the psalmist looks forward to deliverance from the grave. He will not be left there to decay, but God will take him to his heavenly abode. Dahood goes so far as to find here a hope of David that he would be translated like Enoch and Elijah.[5] It would seem enough to hold with Peter that David was a prophet and that he looked for the Messiah to come, confident that the Messiah would not be overpowered by death but would win the victory for his people. If David had hope of his own resurrection (Ps 17:15), much more could he understand that the Messiah (who would die, Ps 22:15) would not be left in the grave. Of course, this is the whole point of Peter's reference in Acts 2:25–31, and of Paul's in Acts 13:35–7.

This verse is used as a proof from the Old Testament that Christ would rise bodily from the grave.

There are a number of passages in Isaiah using Sheol that are thought by some to refer to more than the grave. These have been discussed by Heidel.[6] The passages are in chapters 5,14,28 and 38. Isaiah 5:14 is inconclusive. From the context, either 'the grave' or 'hell' or 'the underworld' would fit. It simply says that Sheol is insatiable.

There are three verses in Isaiah 14 that use Sheol (vv. 9,11,15). The passage is the taunt song against the king of Babylon (vv. 4–23). It is highly poetic and pictures the fall of the king and his reception by kings already dead who marvel at his fall. The lands are at peace since his fall (v. 8). The picture continues in vv. 9–10. The NIV says the 'spirits of the departed' are roused to meet him. The word translated 'spirits' is *repha'im*, which in a number of other places merely means 'dead ones', for example, Isaiah 26:19; Psalm 88:10. In any case the king of Babylon has been brought down to Sheol, where maggots and worms cover him (v. 11). As in Ezekiel 32:27, the grave is here described. Further, in vv. 15–20, where the king is brought down to Sheol to the depths of the pit (or side of the pit [*bor*; see above]), the description gives the treatment of his corpse. He is cast out of his tomb (*qeber*, v. 19); he is covered with the slain and his corpse trampled underfoot as if he had died in battle. He will not be buried (*qeburah*, the participle of *qabar*). These descriptions, with this association with the clear word, *qeber* ('grave'), show that the picture of dead kings rising to meet the fallen king of Babylon is a personification of these earlier kings (who are said to lie in state in their tombs, v. 18) and not a literal description of the condition of the wicked dead.

The other instances in Isaiah do not add greatly to the picture. Isaiah 28:15,18 concerns the coming Assyrian invasion. Those in Jerusalem, like Ahaz who favoured giving tribute to the Assyrians, expected to be spared because of their pact with the invaders. Isaiah in scorn calls it a covenant with death and with Sheol, but declares it will be of no avail. It is actually a covenant with idols (v. 15), and God will punish them. But note the parallel of Sheol and death that is also used elsewhere (1 Sam 2:6; cf. the associations in Ezek 31:14–15). This is in reality a covenant that brings death and that leads to the grave.

Hezekiah's prayer of thanks in Isaiah 38 uses Sheol twice. In v. 10 he says he had faced a premature death and was delivered. In vv. 17–19 he was kept from the 'pit of destruction', which we argued above refers to the decay of the grave. Verse 18 continues: 'Sheol cannot praise you, death [note the parallel] cannot sing your praise . . .' If Sheol here refers to the place of departed spirits, the natural conclusion is soul sleep – or even extinction. But if Sheol here is no more than the grave, then obviously the corpses are silent, though other considerations teach us that the spirits of believers live with God. The last passage in Isaiah (57:9) is in a context that is not clear. It may be only a figurative reference to Israel's extreme efforts to get help, or, more likely, it may refer to her supplications to idols referred to in sarcasm as in Isaiah 38:10,18.

There are a number of passages in Proverbs on which Dahood has shed new light.[7] To begin with, there are the two verses where Sheol and Abaddon are parallel (Prov 15:11; 27:20), as they are in Job 26:6. We have already noted the parallel between *qeber* ('the grave') and Abaddon in Psalm 88:11. The implication is that in all these passages the subject is the tomb. The idea of Proverbs 27:20 that the grave is insatiable is repeated in 30:16; cf. Habakkuk 2:5. Probably the intention of the robbers in Proverbs 1:12 does not go beyond the killing of their innocent victims.

There is another and significant strain best seen in Proverbs 12:28. 'Life' for the righteous is said to be 'no-death' (*'al-mawet*). A very close Ugaritic parallel shows that this expression, 'no-death', is 'eternal life' (NIV 'immortality') – such as the gods of Ugarit claimed to have.[8] A similar verse is 11:19, where the righteous man attains life (Dahood: 'eternal life') while the sinner goes to his death. Again Proverbs 15:24 contrasts the 'path of life' for the wise with Sheol as the alternative. If 'life' in such passages means life beyond the grave, then the 'death' and 'grave' threatened also probably mean more than physical death. The contrast is further drawn between the righteous, who have hope, and the wicked, who have no hope but whose lamp will be snuffed out (Prov 24:14; 23:18; 24:20; 11:7; 13:9; and the similar verses 13:14 and 14:27). In 13:14 and 14:27, the 'fountain of life' for the wise is in contrast with the 'snares of death' for the wicked. Again, if life here is spiritual, death probably is too. As a result we may say that those several verses in Proverbs that threaten death for the wicked may actually speak of spiritual death, and the terms *mawet* and Sheol are used. The result of adultery, death (*mawet*) and the grave (Sheol), may be such a usage (Prov 5:5; 7:27; 9:18 – *repha'im* here parallels Sheol – 16:25). Similar is the passage in Proverbs 23:13. Discipline saves from death, from Sheol. Again, if 'life' means eternal life, 'death' and Sheol in such passages include more than death and more than the grave. Perhaps in these passages the NIV could have used the term 'heaven' for 'life' and 'hell' for 'death' or 'Sheol'. The case, however, is possibly not certain enough or widely enough admitted to go this far. But in every case where Sheol is used the footnote indicates the Hebrew term, and the reader can judge for himself from the context.

The passages in Job are a special case, because it may be argued that Job's perception of the grave and the future life grew as he faced his trial and argued with his comforters.[9] At first Job longed for death and the grave as a respite from his suffering. He uses the word *qeber* ('tomb'), not Sheol (Job 3:11–23). In his second speech he still prefers death (7:15). He declares that the one who 'goes down to Sheol' returns no more (7:9), and in this context says he will soon 'lie down in the dust' and be no more (7:21). To go to Sheol is to lie in the dust and never return. The meaning 'grave' fits Sheol here. Surely the place of departed spirits is not what Job is looking for. In similar vein in Job 10:19–22, Job looks for the grave. The word *qeber* ('tomb') is used, not Sheol. He calls the grave a place of no return, a land of gloom and deep shadow, of disorder where the light is like darkness. This does not describe the place of departed spirits or an underworld. The description is that of *qeber*, the grave. The passage teaches us that similar references to Sheol elsewhere also mean no more than the darkness, dissolution and dust of the tomb.

A new element enters in Job's discourse in chapter 14. Here he protests man's frailty and contrasts man with the hope for a tree that 'sends up a new sprout' when it is cut down. Man is different. First he says that man never rises (v. 12). Then he longs to be hidden in the grave (Sheol) till God's anger passes and he remembers Job (v. 13). But he must raise again, and insistently, the question of resurrection (v. 14a). Finally, in hope he says he will wait for his new sprout to come. God will call and Job will answer. God will care for his child much more than for the senseless tree (vv. 14b–15). Job's hope at times grew dim, but he never lost his faith in a good and just God. Nor could he admit that he suffered for some great sin. If he felt the injustice in this world, he was forced to consider a world to come in which injustice would be rectified. Job 17:11–16 probably carries on this same vein. He faces the grave, Sheol, and its corruption (*shaḥat*). If this is all, he says, where is my hope? But Job has a hope (Job 16:17–21). The poignancy of Job's question shows that he hopes for more than the grave (Sheol) and its dust (17:16). His hope, as he had said in 14:15, is for a future where God would call him to a new life.

This hope is made explicit in Job's famous declaration of 19:25–7. The details of this passage are difficult, but the conclusion is plain. Job gives a testimony that he wants to outlast time (v. 24). He knows that his Redeemer (*go'el*, 'vindicator') lives – his Redeemer is surely the living God – and that at last he will stand upon 'dust' (*'aphar*). 'Earth' is not the usual nuance of this word. Dahood has shown that pronouns in poetry often do double duty.[10] In this context the implication is that God will stand 'upon my dust'. The next line is the most obscure. The natural sense of the words is: 'And after my skin this has been struck off.' Some interpret it: 'After someone has struck off (or destroyed) this my skin.' However, Hebrew prefers a different construction for a temporal clause: the preposition followed by the infinitive, then the subject of the infinitive. If *'ori* ('my skin') is taken instead as the infinitive of the verb *'ur* ('to awake, arise'; cf. Job 14:12), then the grammar is natural and the sense is easy: 'And after I awake.' The following 'this', which is feminine – probably abstract feminine – refers to his disease or his circumstance: 'And after I awake, when this disease has been taken away, from my flesh I shall see God.' The emphasis points, contrary to some critical assertions, to Job's confidence in a physical resurrection: 'I myself will see him, with my own eyes – I and not another.' Sheol is not used in this famous passage, but it is an important passage to show the progress in Job's thought and the heights of hope to which he attains. Job goes on to refer to the case of the wicked. He says the problem is that they go to the grave, Sheol, in peace (21:13), but he declares that God will bring calamity upon them at last (21:17, 30). In 24:19 the grave, Sheol, takes the sinners (note that the worm feeds on them, as so often in the description of the grave), but God's eyes are on their ways and he will give them what they deserve (24:21–4).

There are a few other passages that use Sheol in some figurative or illustrative sense and do not add much to the argument already given. Some of them would be applicable whether Sheol were taken as the grave, hell or the underworld. Sheol is used, for example, as a symbol of depth as opposed to height. Job 11:8 ('higher than heaven, deeper than Sheol') is a case in point. Psalm 139:8 is another: 'If I go up to the heavens . . . if I make my bed in the depths [Sheol].' Compare also Amos 9:2: 'down to the depths of the grave [Sheol]' or 'up to the heavens'. Deuteronomy 32:22 is similar but lacks the reference to the heavens above: 'a fire . . . that burns to the realm of death [Sheol] below.' Psalm 86:13 also lacks the reference to heaven: 'You have delivered me from the depths of the grave [Sheol below].'

Of all these passages we may say that there is no

indication that Sheol is a very deep place. The Hebrews had no deep mines or oil wells. They dug wells some distance down, but a dug tomb was to them a good symbol of death. The parallel to Sheol in Deuteronomy 32:22 is the 'foundations of the mountains', not some mythical place. Psalm 86:13 uses the same expression that is applied to the 'earth below' in Ezekiel 32:24, and the thing spoken of there is clearly a grave, as the word *qeber* in the context shows. A very similar expression is used for the word 'pit' in Psalm 88:6; yet as already noted, the context of v. 5 shows that a grave (*qeber*) is intended. In the Amos passage, the other expression for height is the 'top of Carmel', and the parallel for depth is the bottom of the sea. It was from the depths of the sea that Jonah cried and was delivered (Jonah 2:2; cf. v. 6, which speaks of the roots of the mountains). Surely these are observable extremes that do not point to an underworld for Sheol. They are satisfied by the meaning 'grave'.

The remaining symbolic poetic passages speak of the greed or dominance or dangers of Sheol. The Song of Songs says that love is as strong as death, its jealousy (or ardour) as unyielding as the grave (Sheol; 8:6). Note the common parallel of death and Sheol. The sorrows, cords or pains of Sheol are mentioned in Psalm 18:5, in its parallel (2 Sam 22:6) and in the passage probably dependent on these (Ps 116:3). They are highly poetic references that could fit either grave, underworld or hell.

It would seem that when all these references are considered, the translation 'grave' is the most appropriate one. Death comes to all. The grave is never full. The ancient grave was a pit below the surface of the earth. It was characterised by dust, darkness and decay. The body there lies still and eventually forgotten by all except its Maker. But death and the grave will one day be overcome by the one who brought life and immortality to light through the gospel. This element of the gospel was also known in type and shadow before its great fulfilment. That the Hebrews believed in some underworld like that of the ancient Near East cannot be got from the Bible. Soul sleep also is to be rejected. There are places, however, especially in Proverbs, where the word may be used in a fuller sense, as the word 'life' seems to be. In such contexts the grave and death may well stand for eternal death, the result of unrepented sin.

There are two passages remaining to be considered. The first is the hopeless remark of Ecclesiastes 9:10. If here Sheol means only grave, the remark is true. The body there ceases from labour and thought. But perhaps we should not too much depend on this verse, as it might only express one of the false philosophies Solomon raises only to discard in favour of his ultimate *summum bonum* expressed in 12:13.

The other and last passage is Hosea 13:14: 'I will ransom them from the power of the grave [Sheol; cf. the discussion of Ps 49:7,15 above]; I will redeem them from death [*mawet*]. Where, O death [*mawet*], are your plagues? Where, O grave [Sheol], is your destruction?' It will not do to say that the grave is only a symbol of Israel's captivity. The emphasis in the context is on Ephraim, and though they were carried away for their sin, their return is not held out as a hope. Rather, this treatment of death matches the verse of Isaiah (25:8) studied above: 'he will swallow up death for ever' (or 'in victory' – the Hebrew will bear either meaning). It is highly significant that Paul put these two verses together in his long defence of the bodily resurrection in 1 Corinthians 15:54–5. In the Old Testament, as in the New, the ultimate hope is the redemption of our bodies (Rom 8:23) when the sorrow of death and the pain of parting will be no more. When the Sadducees denied this, Jesus said that they greatly erred, not knowing the Old Testament Scriptures or the power of God.

There are many verses beyond the scope of this study that deal with that time when God will wipe away all tears from all faces. The catena in Isaiah begins at the resurrection passage in 25:8 and carries through 35:10; 51:3,11; 60:20 to the new heavens and earth in 65:17–19. Then the pains, fears, tears, darkness, oblivion, and dust of Sheol will be no more, and those who are wise will shine like the stars for ever and ever. But there is a dark side. For the wicked, the graves indeed will be opened, but to everlasting contempt – of which there is solemn warning also in the end of Isaiah (66:24) as well as in the words of Christ (Mark 9:48): 'their worm does not die and the fire is not quenched.'

NOTES

1 A. Cowley, *Aramaic Papyri of the Fifth Century* BC (Oxford, 1923), No. 71, p. 15.
2 Mitchell Dahood, *Psalms III*, The Anchor Bible (Garden City, NY: Doubleday, 1970), pp. XLI–LII.
3 Mitchell Dahood, *Psalms 1 1–50*, The Anchor Bible (Garden City, NY: Doubleday, 1966), p. 132.
4 Ibid., p. 91.
5 Ibid.
6 Alexander Heidel, *The Gilgamesh Epic and Old Testament Parallels* (Chicago: University of Chicago Press, 1949), pp. 137–223.
7 Mitchell Dahood, *Proverbs and Northwest Semitic Philology* (Rome: Pontifical Biblical Institute, 1963).
8 Cyrus H. Gordon, *Ugaritic Textbook* (Rome: Pontifical Biblical Institute, 1965), p. 248 (2 Aqht VI: 27–8).
9 R. Laird Harris, 'The Book of Job and Its Doctrine of God', *Presbuterion: Covenant Seminary Review* 7/1–2 (Spring–Fall 1981): 5–33.
10 Dahood, *Psalms III*, p. 429.

6 WHEN THE SPIRIT WAS POETIC

John H. Stek

The Committee on Bible Translation decided early on, in setting translation policy for the NIV, that biblical poetry should be translated and printed as poetry. That decision occasioned little discussion and was made without debate. It seemed self-evident that biblical poetry should be presented to the reader as poetry. Moreover, the policy was not innovative; it had already been adopted by the committees that produced the Revised Version of 1881 (New Testament) and 1885 (Old Testament) and the American Standard Version of 1901.[1] Also the translators of the Revised Standard Version (1952) had chosen to follow the same policy and had carried it out even more thoroughly.[2]

But what does it mean to translate and print biblical poetry as poetry? To this, too, not much discussion was devoted – which may cause readers of the NIV some wonderment, especially since poetry is notoriously 'untranslatable'. The reason, however, is well known to every student of ancient Hebrew literature. Detailed theoretical discussions would have involved the translators in such a morass of uncertainties that actual translation would have been stalled at the beginning. Not that biblical poetry is unintelligible, but the theory of ancient Hebrew poetry is still too little known.

Although the Israelites made extensive use of poetry and developed it to a high art, they did not subject it to close formal analysis. Consequently, they have not served us with theoretical reflections on their poetic forms, as did the Greeks. We are left to study their compositions without the aid of their own understanding of their poets' craft. Such early analyses as we do have are attempts to apply Greek theory to Semitic poetry, which is about as useful as attempting to grade eggs on a device designed to grade oranges.

Since the publication of Bishop Lowth's lectures on Hebrew poetry,[3] it has become a commonplace to acknowledge that the most distinctive characteristic of biblical poetry (that which sets it off from biblical prose) is parallelism. It had, of course, long been recognised that ancient Israelite poetry did not employ rhyme. But assuming on the basis of classical Greek models that all poetry must be metrical, endless attempts had been made (from at least the first century AD) to discover the metrical patterns of the Hebrew poetic tradition. Every attempt had foundered, however, on the intransigence of the text to yield to such analysis. This fact, too, Lowth recognised – though he continued to believe that Hebrew poetry must have been governed by some kind of (now recoverable) metrical scheme. No one could miss the terseness of Hebrew poetry, nor the pervasive vividness of its imagery, its profusion of similes and metaphors or the uniqueness of its vocabulary, abounding in unusual words and syntax and in archaic forms – all contributing to an impassioned, elevated style. But style alone seemed insufficient to mark off poetry from prose. Lowth therefore fixed on parallelism as the one distinguishing criterion and argued his case so persuasively that even now his work is honoured as the cornerstone of all that is sure in the theory of biblical poetry.[4]

The Hebrew poetic line is ordinarily binary (occasionally trinary), with the two half-lines relatively balanced (though the first is frequently somewhat longer than the second).[5] Lowth designated the relationship between the half-lines 'parallelism' and developed a simple classification to cover all instances. In many lines the second half more or less echoes the first, as:

> Rescue me, O LORD, from evil men:
>> protect me from men of violence.
>>> (Ps 140:1)

This Lowth called 'synonymous parallelism'. On the other hand, in a large number of cases the second express a contrast to the first, for which Psalm 138:6 offers a good example:

> Though the LORD is on high, he looks upon the lowly,
>> but the proud he knows from afar.

Lowth's apt classification for this relationship was 'antithetic parallelism'. However, many lines fit neither of these categories since the second half of the line neither echoes the first nor contrasts with it but in various ways advances the thought or even completes the syntax of the first, as:

> May all the kings of the earth praise you, O LORD,
>> when they hear the words of your
>>> mouth.
>>>> (Ps 138:5)

For this category Lowth chose the elastic term 'synthetic parallelism' since it had to be flexible enough to cover all instances that did not fit well under the other two.

The virtue of Lowth's analysis lay in its focus on parallelism as the key feature of biblical poetry and in the simplicity of its classification. He was a persuasive voice against the all too easy (and ages-old) assumption that the prosody of Greek classical poetry provided the standards by which all good poetry is to be scanned. His work also cleared the ground for recognising poetry where it occurs in the narrative books and in the prophets.[6]

Lowth's work did not bring to an end the search for some kind of controlling metrical scheme in Hebrew poetry. Impressed by the terseness and general symmetry of the Hebrew poetic line, later scholars continued to make valiant attempts to discover the system of scansion that must have served the poets as formal restraints. Their concerns were not only aesthetic. Exegetically it is important to know precisely where a line begins and ends and just where the caesura falls that separates the half-lines. Those whose researches need to be mentioned here are Julius Ley,[7] Carl Budde,[8] Eduard Sievers,[9] and George Buchanan Gray.[10] What has endured from their studies is the practice of counting primary accents (or significant words) as a measure of a poetic line and its half-lines. On this system the most common lines are 3/2, 3/3, 4/3, 4/4, and 2/2. More recently the proposal has been made that such scansion ought to be supplemented by syllable count as an additional (indirect) method for measuring the metrical limits employed by the Hebrew poets.[11]

Lowth's threefold classification of types of parallelism has also been subsequently elaborated. The most enduring contribution has been that of G. B. Gray.[12] In addition to recognising Lowth's antithetic and synthetic[13] parallelisms, he identified three categories, which he offered as a refinement on Lowth's 'synonymous parallelism' – and to a degree on Lowth's 'synthetic parallelism'. These he designated 'complete parallelism', 'incomplete parallelism with compensation' and 'incomplete parallelism without compensation'. In the first of these, each term of the first half-line has its parallel in the second, either in the same order, as in:

> By-the-breath   of-God   they-perish,
> and-by-the-blast   of-his-anger
>   are-they-consumed.
>
> (Job 4:9)[14]

or in different order, as in:

> And-he-shall-smite   the-violent   with-the-rod
>   of-his-mouth,

and-with-the-breath   of-his-lips   shall-he-slay
the-wicked.

(Isa 11:4)

When two half-lines have the same number of terms but only some are parallel, the parallelism is 'incomplete with compensation', as in:

Her-hand   to-the-tent-peg   she-stretched-forth,
and-her-right-hand   to-the-workman's   mallet.

(Judg 5:26)

If two half-lines have a different number of terms but those present in the shorter of the two all have their parallels in the longer, the parallelism is 'incomplete without compensation', as in:

I-will-restore   thy-judges   as-at-the-first,
and-thy-counsellors   as-at-the-beginning.

(Isa 1:26)

The above is a brief indication of the (rather elementary) theoretical tradition concerning Hebrew poetry within which the translators of the NIV approached the biblical texts. That in application judgments were often difficult and decisions frequently not unanimous will not surprise those who have worked with the original texts. It ought to be noted here, however, that temptations to emend the text to fit poetic theory were rigorously resisted.

One of the more perplexing questions facing biblical translators is the judgment as to what is poetic and what is not. The problem is especially acute in the narrative books, the Latter Prophets, and the Letters. Does the mere presence of parallelism infallibly signify poetry? And given the fact that 'parallelism' is frequently 'formal' or 'merely rhythmical', can the presence of terse, balanced clauses serve as sufficient indicators of the poetic? Did the biblical writers even work with a clear and sharp distinction between prose and poetry, or was there for them only a continuum between the 'poetic' and the 'prosaic'? In view of these uncertainties, the NIV translators chose to print as 'poetry' whatever line appeared in their judgment to sufficiently reflect characteristics found in the known poetry – without attempting to distinguish definitively between poetry and elevated prose. Hence readers of the NIV should not be surprised to find such a passage as Genesis 9:6 scanned as 'poetry' – and Genesis 12:2–3; 15:1; 16:11–12; 24:60; Exodus 32:18; Leviticus 10:3; Numbers 10:35–6; 12:6–8; Deuteronomy 7:10; Judges 16:24; 1 Samuel 15:33 . . . and Philippians 2:6–11; 1 John 2:12–14.

Once the determination was made to translate a passage as 'poetry', a few basic rules governed: (1) Keep the style tight, economical (but do not attempt to imitate the terseness of Hebrew); (2) use the normal idiom and style of the NIV as much as possible (do not follow the Hebrew tendency to employ archaisms and other unusual words and grammar); (3) retain the vivid imagery of the original except where it might obscure meaning; (4) strive for a flowing (but irregular) rhythm to facilitate oral reading and memorisation; (5) avoid rhyme; (6) wherever possible, consistent with good style, reflect in translation the limits and sequence of the half-lines; and (7) print the second (and third) line segments below the first with slight indentation. Occasionally, where the English rendering of a Hebrew half-line was necessarily so long as to necessitate a run-on line even in the single column editions, the translators divided the line and printed it as two half-lines. For example, the following represents a single two-segment line in Hebrew:

> I will take away its hedge,
>> and it will be destroyed;
> I will break down its wall,
>> and it will be trampled.
>> (Isa 5:5)

Psalm 2:2 is a single three-segment line, but NIV renders it:

> The kings of the earth take their stand
> > and the rulers gather together
> against the LORD
> > and against his Anointed One.

Purists may object, but the frequency of run-on lines could thus be reduced – as well as the number of awkward breaks determined only by the printer's calculations.

Uncertainties concerning the line structure of Hebrew poetry are not the end of the translator's difficulties. Equally uncertain is the question of stanza formation, that is, the construction of poetic units larger than the line that are designed to give form to a composition. There can be no doubt that Hebrew poets often composed couplets:

> In you our fathers put their trust;
> > they trusted and you delivered them.
> They cried to you and were saved;
> > in you they trusted and were not disappointed.
> > > (Ps 22:4–5)

> The LORD foils the plans of the nations;
> > he thwarts the purposes of the
> > > peoples.
> But the plans of the LORD stand firm for ever,
> > the purposes of his heart through all
> > > generations.
> > > > (Ps 33:10–11)

But did they use larger units as deliberate structural constraints? Examples offered by some of the alphabetic acrostics (Pss 37; 119; Lam 1; 2; 3; 4), by psalms containing recurring refrains (42–3; 46; 49; 57; 80 – also Isa 9:8–10:4), and by others that show thematic progression at regular intervals (such as Pss 2; 3; 38; 41; 94; 101; 110; 113; 125; 130; 149) have suggested to some that stanza formation must have been an integral part of the Hebrew poetic tradition. Here once again the models of classical poetry (and other non-Semitic literary traditions) have beclouded the issue. Studies based on them have been generally recognised as wrong-headed, however. Early in this century Gray announced that his discussion of stanzas in Hebrew poetry could be brief 'because what can be safely said here does not require many words to state it, and what has been both unsafely and erroneously asserted has already received, perhaps, sufficient refutation from other writers'.[15] He acknowledged that evidences of regular stanza formation are occasionally present, and 'the regular recurrence of *equal* sections in any considerable poem cannot easily be attributed to accident',[16] but he insisted that 'poems in which the greater sense-divisions, though well-marked, consist of a varying number of distichs [binary lines] must be considered to have been written free from the restraint of any strophic [stanzaic] law; in this case, if we use the term strophe [stanza], it must mean simply a verse paragraph of indeterminate length uncontrolled by any formal artistic scheme'.[17]

Mid-century, T. H. Robinson was still seconding Gray's judgment. While admitting that 'strophic [stanzaic] arrangement is obvious in certain cases', he felt constrained to add:

> We can however, recognise a formal strophic arrangement only when certain conditions are fulfilled. There must be a real division in sense between the sections, and they must show some regularity, either uniformity or at least symmetry, in the length of the 'strophes'. In other cases we must assume that we have merely verse paragraphs, which are inevitable except in short poems, and are no part of the formal structure [. . .] We must rest content with the fact that while a stanza arrangement may be found in a number of Hebrew poems, it is not an essential element in poetic form.[18]

Since the judgment that regular stanza formation was not an 'essential element' (however occasionally present) in

100

Hebrew poetic form has been shared by most biblical scholars in this century, the NIV translators chose not to pursue detailed investigations of that matter. Instead, they opted for the less controversial general policy of marking off verse paragraphs by spacing. It was recognised, however, that certain other factors ought to be taken into account as an aid to the readers. The conventions of the prayer psalms, for example, called for the use of a variety of modes of speech, each with its own distinct function. Common among these are: initial appeal to God; descriptions of distress or need (lament); protestations of innocence or confessions of sin; expressions of confidence that God will hear and deliver; petitions for deliverance, help or forgiveness; indictments of enemies; calls for redress; vows to praise (for answer to prayer). Each of these, it was judged, should be set off by spaces, even if a particular function was represented by only a single line. The brief prayer found in Psalm 54 provides a convenient illustration:

1 Save me, O God, by your name;
           vindicate me by your might.
2 Hear my prayer, O God;
           listen to the words of my mouth.

3 Strangers are attacking me;
           ruthless men seek my life –
           men without regard for God.

4 Surely God is my help;
           the LORD is the one who sustains me.

5 Let evil recoil on those who slander me;
           in your faithfulness destroy them.

6 I will sacrifice a freewill offering to you;
           I will praise your name, O LORD, for it is
                 good.
7 For he has delivered me from all my troubles,
           and my eyes have looked in triumph on my
                 foes.

Clearly this short psalm gives no indication of regular stanza formation. Nor does it contain verse paragraphs extending beyond the line except in the opening and closing couplets. But the prayer is composed of five distinct functional units. Verses 1–2 constitute the initial appeal to God for deliverance. Verse 3 describes the need (with indictment of the enemy interwoven as a secondary theme: 'ruthless . . . men without regard for God'). In v. 4 we hear a confession of confidence. This is followed in v. 5 by a call for redress. The closing couplet (vv. 6–7) develops the vow to praise for deliverance. Readers of the NIV should be alert to this additional function of spacing.

Still another feature of the Psalms came to light in the course of translating. A number of them contain a one-line introduction and/or conclusion. Those with both may serve as illustrations: 8; 15; 64; 82; 111; 112; 118; 146 (29 has an introduction and conclusion each composed of couplets).[19] Here, too, spacing was used to set these off from the body of the psalm.

The reader may recall that both Gray and Robinson had concluded that where the verse paragraphs are made up of varied numbers of lines they are 'uncontrolled by any formal artistic scheme'.[20] That judgment needs qualification. Since the 1950s many studies of individual psalms have appeared that focus on stylistics. Several of these have called attention to architectonic structures that indicate deliberate design governing whole poems. Such self-conscious forms had been long recognised in the alphabetic acrostic poems. But now new, more intricate and creative forms began to come to light. One of the leaders in this research was Dr Nic. H. Ridderbos of the Free University in Amsterdam. In 1963 he published an article devoted mainly to the stylistics of Psalms 22, 25 and 45.[21] In it, however, he briefly called attention to the unique structure of Psalms 44 and 9. Of the latter he only observed that it falls into two halves of precisely ten lines each.[22] But his analysis of Psalm 44 disclosed a far more complex structure. An initial 'hymn' of ten lines (vv. 1–8) is followed successively by a complaint of eight lines (vv. 9–16), a protestation of innocence developed in six lines (vv. 17–22), and a prayer of four lines (vv. 23–6). Ridderbos likened the structure to a ziggurat (a Mesopotamian stepped pyramid crowned by a sanctuary) which the poet mounted, as it were, in order to present his prayer to God.[23] In his later commentary he carried the analysis further, noting that each of the stages of the pyramid is constructed of precisely-balanced halves so that the stanza structure is that of 5–5—4–4—3–3—2–2 lines.[24]

The significance of such studies lies in their disclosure that the Biblical poets often chose to compose under the artistic restraints of architectonic designs. Psalm 54, discussed above, reflects such design. A pair of couplets (vv. 1–2, 6–7) frame the prayer; vv. 3 and 5 are thematically linked as indictment of the enemy and call for redress; and at the centre (v. 4) stands an expression of confidence. Psalm 10 contains in vv. 2–11 the classic (for the Psalter) description of 'the wicked'. This ten-line stanza falls thematically into two balanced parts of five lines each: The first describes the arrogance of 'the wicked' (vv. 2–6) while the second describes his immorality (vv. 7–11). Notice that the concluding line of each half quotes the wicked: 'He says to himself, ". . ."' (Perhaps the stanza should have been divided into two, since the succeeding stanza [vv. 12–15] is also a unit of five lines.) Another clear example is Psalm 29. As in Psalm 54, couplets (vv. 1–2, 10–11) frame the whole. The body of the psalm is a seven-line hymn celebrating 'the voice of the LORD'.[25] Psalm 110 is composed of two precisely balanced stanzas,[26] each introduced by a two-line oracle.

A more complicated architecture is to be found in vv. 1–26 of Psalm 104. Following a one-line introduction (v. 1) that announces the main theme (and should have been set off by spacing), the author composed a hymn to the Creator with a concentric stanza structure of 3–5–9–5–3 lines consecutively. In the first (vv. 2–4), he celebrates the majesty of God as displayed in the celestial realm; in the second (vv. 5–9), he praises God for making the foundations and boundaries of the earth (dry land) secure; in the third (vv.

10–18 – the centre), we hear him rejoicing over God's gift of water to various types of geographical regions so that life flourishes in them all; in the fourth (vv. 19–23), he celebrates God's secure ordering of days and seasons, fitting them to the ways of the wild and of man; in the fifth (vv. 24–6), he summarises (v. 24) and then concludes the theme he has been developing by joyfully noting how God has even domesticated the awesome marine realm – so that life flourishes within it, ships sail securely upon it, and the fearsome leviathan is but a playful creature frolicking in it.

It is to be observed that this portion of the psalm is thematically as well as structurally concentric. The first and fifth stanzas speak respectively of the celestial and marine realms, the two great cosmic realms that were perceived by the ancients to frame 'the earth'. Stanzas two and four celebrate the security of the structures of space (earth) and time (days and seasons) in the arena of (earthly) life. At the centre the poet devotes his praise to God's varied yet bountiful supply of water with which he blesses life. Here, too, a concentric pattern is employed. The first three lines (vv. 10–12) signalise God's provision of water in semi-arid regions (through springs, as in the Negev), the second three (vv. 13–15) his supply of water for cultivated regions (through rain, as in the 'mountains' of Judah and Ephraim), the final three (vv. 16–18) his abundant watering of the high mountain regions (such as Lebanon). Manifestly, the poet stood on the 'mountains of Israel' to survey all the works of the Creator, and the architecture of his hymn reflects both the scope and the perspective of his vision.[27]

Psalm 132 offers yet another striking example of architectonics that emerged in the process of translation. It is evident that the heart of the psalm is a prayer for a king of the house of David (probably an enthronement prayer) and God's reassuring answer (possibly spoken by a priest). Petition proper, however, is limited to vv. 1 and 10. This distribution is not haphazard. Each line of petition is followed by two four-line stanzas precisely similar in form, namely, an introductory line leading into a three-line

quotation. The two stanzas following the first line of petition recall David's commitment to the Lord and to his
(proposed) temple, while those following the second line of
petition recall the Lord's commitment to David and to
Jerusalem (the city of the temple). The couplet with which
the psalm concludes (vv. 17–18) constitutes God's answer
to the two-line petition.[28] Thus both prayer and answer
have been provided a larger setting within the context of
the Yahweh–David relationship. And the symmetries of
that relationship have been highlighted by the architectonic
symmetries of the psalm.

We may further note that in this psalm a couplet of
petition has been split up and separated by inserted
material (the two stanzas in vv. 2–9), and is then separated
from the couplet in which it receives its answer by
additional inserted material (the two stanzas in vv. 11–16).
Such interruptions are found elsewhere. Psalm 77 displays
a symmetrical structure following its two-line introduction
(vv. 1–2) in that the stanzas have been given a 4–3–3–4
pattern. But inserted between the third and fourth lines of
the last of these[29] stands a four-line stanza that is both
thematically and structurally distinct. Between the line that
recalls the exodus from Egypt and that which recalls the
desert wanderings of Israel, the poet interrupts the syntax
of his reminiscence to evoke memory of the awesome
epiphany which opened a way through the sea for Yahweh
(and Israel) to pass. In this inserted stanza all the lines are
extended to three segments (or tristichs, as they are often
called).

Another instance of an interrupted stanza is found in
Amos 5:1–17, though there it is part of a far more intricate
structure.[30] The section is occasionally interrupted by prose
introductions (in vv. 1, 3, 4, 16), but these can for purposes
of analysis be ignored. The passage is framed by references
to lamentation over the fall of Israel (vv. 2–3, 16–17).[31]
Within this frame, the call to 'seek . . . and live' found in vv.
4–6 is taken up again in vv. 14–15 – thus yielding an A–B
. . . B–A thematic pattern. Up to this point the structure is

rather straightforward and unproblematic – and is duplicated elsewhere. But if one attempts to read vv. 7–13 as
thematically continuous, one meets with apparent confusion. The syntax of v. 7 is obviously not continued until v.
10. Between them lies a hymnic celebration of the majesty
of Yahweh, who governs the celestial realm (v. 8) and on
earth brings destruction on strongholds (v. 9). But neither is
the syntax of v. 10 continued in v. 11. In Hebrew, vv. 7 and
10 are written in third-person forms while vv. 11–12a
employ second-person forms. Third-person forms are not
resumed until v. 12b. Hence it appears evident that a stanza
of explicit indictment ('You . . . you . . . you . . .') has been
inserted between the second (v. 10) and third (v. 12b) lines
of implicit indictment (in Hebrew: 'Those who . . . who . . .
who . . .') just as a hymnic stanza evoking Yahweh's majesty has been inserted between its first (v. 7) and second
(v. 10) lines. Thematically, therefore, the A–B . . . B–A
thematic pattern of vv. 1–6, 14–17, noted above, frames an
implicit indictment of Israel set forth in a four-line stanza
(vv. 7, 10, 12b, 13):

7   Those who turn justice into bitterness
          and cast righteousness to the ground,
      . . .
10   hate the one who reproves in court
          and despises him who tells the truth.
      . . .
12b They oppress the righteous and take bribes
          and deprive the poor of justice in the courts.
13   Therefore the prudent man keeps quiet in such times,
          for the times are evil.

(Because this constitutes at least an implicit indictment, the
NIV translators have transposed to second-person forms –
as was done elsewhere where the Hebrew and English
idioms do not naturally coincide.) Within this stanza, the
author has made two insertions by which he sets starkly
side by side an evocation of Yahweh's awful majesty and an

explicit indictment of Israel's awful sin. The dramatic effect is heightened when we observe that the interrupted stanza may be Amos's own reflection on the situation (note that he, in distinction from Yahweh, is the speaker in v. 6 and again in vv. 14–15), but the hymn (vv. 8–9) introduces Yahweh's presence into that scene, and vv. 11–12a voice Yahweh's own indictment (see the 'I know . . .' of v. 12a).

If this seems excessively complicated, it must be remembered that the biblical poets were highly skilled in a literary art that had been developing for millennia, and their readers were practised in discerning poetic subtleties. What is more, while we wish to catch the full sense on the run, the authors of the Scriptures obviously expected their writings to receive deliberate and studied attention.

One further poetic structural feature that came to light in translating may be mentioned here – and that will have to suffice for the present purpose. As was noted above, Psalm 54 has a concentric structure with an expression of confidence located at the centre of the prayer. This was not the only psalm with a significant line precisely centred. One finds such centring also in Psalms 42–3; 47 (a couplet); 48; 86 (a triplet); 92 (but the stanza analysis of this psalm is open to question); 138 (a couplet); and 141.[32] These centres have been set off by spacing.

Of special interest is the instance in Psalm 42–3. Although this is divided into two psalms in both the Hebrew and Septuagint text traditions, it has long been recognised that these were originally one. In fact, because of the recurring refrain, appeal has often been made to this (combined) psalm as evidence of regular stanza formation in the Hebrew poetic tradition. It has, however, been somewhat of an embarrassment to those seeking evidence of strict regularity in that the second stanza is one line longer than the first and third.[33] But given the frequency of the device of centring, an explanation is at hand. At the very centre of the whole poem (exclusive of the refrains), the author has inserted a centre line – abruptly interrupting the lament theme of vv. 6–7, 9–10 – that expresses the basis for the self-exhortation of the refrains.

Not all the stylistics of the Hebrew poets can be so readily conveyed in translation as those just noted. At times a translation conceals almost as much as it reveals. Alphabetic acrostics, for example, cannot be duplicated. Nor can the Hebrew poet's frequent use of assonance and alliteration. In translation one does not hear again the poignant sounds of Isaiah 24:16–18:

> *razi li razi li*
> > *'oy li*
> *bogedim bagadu*
> > *ubeged bogedim bagadu*
> *pahad wapahat wapah*
>
> . . . .
> . . . . *happahad*
> . . . . *happahat*
> . . . . *happahat*
> . . . . *bappah*[34]

And something of the expressive power of the original is washed when '*tob shem mishshemen tob*' can only be 'literally' rendered 'A good name is better than fine perfume' (Eccles 7:1). The same is true when Isaiah's devastating wordplay at the conclusion of his vineyard song is reduced to 'literal' English:

> And he looked for justice [*mishpat*],
> > but saw bloodshed [*mispah*];
> for righteousness [*sedaqah*],
> > but heard cries of distress [*se'aqah*].
> > > (Isa 5:7)

Similarly lost is the wordplay that links the first line of Psalm 64 with its last line – v. 1 beginning with the verb *shama'* (hear) and v. 10 with the verb *samah* (rejoice).[35]

Yet another feature of Hebrew poetry gets covered over

by the translator's concern for clarity and 'naturalness' of expression. I refer to the frequent practice of the Hebrew poets to capitalise on the conventions of their literary tradition, which allows them to employ unusual word order. Quite literally the line in Psalm 66:16 reads:

> Come and listen,[36] and I will tell you,
>   all you who fear God,
>   what he has done for me.

As can be readily recognised, the vocative 'all you who fear God' belongs syntactically immediately after the exhortation 'come and listen', while the final clause, 'what he has done for me' is the direct object of 'I will tell you'. Hence the transposition of phrases in the NIV rendering:

> Come and listen, all you who fear God;
>   let me tell you what he has done for me.[37]

This ability on the part of the Hebrew poet to interrupt syntactical sequences without confusing his reader[38] at times creates troubling ambiguities for later readers of these texts. A star example is Psalm 87:4. Here a 'literal' rendering yields:

> I-will-record   Rahab   and-Babylon
>   concerning-those-who-acknowledge-me.
>   Behold,   Philistia   and-Tyre
>   with-Cush,
>   This-one   was-born   there   (in Zion).

On the generally accepted assumption that Hebrew idiom never separates *hinneh* ('behold') from the phrase it introduces, this line has universally been interpreted as anticipating the world-wide expansion of the people of God (the citizens of Zion) to include numbers of people from Israel's historic enemies. On this reading, the psalm has

109

been hailed (especially by Christian interpreters) as an extraordinary echo of the anticipatory universalism of some of the prophets (cf., for example, Isa 2:2–4; 19:23–5; 25:6–8; Mic 4:1–3) in sharp contrast to the other Zion songs of the Psalter (cf. Pss 48; 76; 84; 122; 137; see also 42–3; 126; 132). Let Perowne be spokesman for this traditional interpretation. After remarking on Israel's historic 'jealous exclusiveness' and 'feeling of antipathy' towards all her neighbours and the 'corrective' visions of those prophets who foresaw 'Gentiles coming to the light of Jerusalem' and 'a time when all wars and all national antipathies shall cease', and 'the temple of Jehovah [shall become] the centre of a common faith and worship', Perowne observes:

> It is this last hope which expresses itself in this Psalm, but which expresses itself in a form that has no exact parallel in other passages. Foreign nations are here described, not as captives or tributaries, not even as doing voluntary homage to the greatness and glory of Zion, but as actually incorporated and enrolled, by a new birth, among her sons [. . .] God himself receives each one as a child newly born into His family, acknowledges each as His son, and enrols him with His own in the sacred register of His children.
> It is this mode of anticipating a future union and brotherhood of all the nations of the earth, not by a conquest, but by incorporation into one state, and by a birthright so acquired, which is so remarkable [. . .] The Psalm stands alone amongst the writings of the Old Testament, in representing this union of nations as a new birth into the city of God.[39]

It is understandable that interpreters (especially Christian interpreters) might be reluctant to reconsider this 'remarkable' and singular anticipation of New Testament themes in the Old Testament. But evidence for interrupted syntax in Hebrew poetry can hardly be denied. And that raises the possibility of its presence here. Thus the line is open to the reading in which the references to 'Rahab . . . Babylon . . . Philistia . . . Tyre . . . Cush' stand in the vocative and in which the basic syntax of the line is:

> I will record . . . concerning those who acknowledge me
> (as their covenant Lord) –
> > Behold, . . . –
> > 'This one was born there (in Zion).'

This is the alternative possibility represented in the NIV footnote. On this interpretation, the psalm stands with Psalms 48 and 76 in celebrating the impregnable security of Zion, but speaks specifically of the like security of all those whom the Lord records as native-born citizens of his royal city – namely, those of his people who acknowledge him as their covenant Lord.[40]

The possibility of an interrupted syntax following *hinneh* ('behold') is reinforced by what appears to be a similar case in Jeremiah 4:16. There we read:

> Proclaim   to-the-nations – Behold [*hinneh*] –
> > publish to-Jerusalem:
> Besiegers   are-coming   from-a-land
> > that-is-distant,
> > > and-they-utter   against   the-cities-of
> > Judah   their-voice.

Concerning the presence of *hinneh* at the end of the first half-line, John Bright expresses a widely held view: '[It] cannot be correct.'[41] But surely it is better to recognise that while in prose *hinneh* never stands separated from the phrase or clause it introduces, the same restraints were not felt to apply in poetry, and that there *hinneh* anticipates the announcement that follows.[42]

Job 9:19 contains yet another 'anomalous' occurrence of *hinneh*. Literally the text reads:

> If (it is)-a-matter-of-strength, (he is) mighty,
> > > *hinneh* (behold);
> > and-if   a-matter-of-justice, who will-summon-
> > > (or arraign)-him?

111

Although the *hinneh* is widely thought to be a corrupt form here also,[43] the line may better be viewed as containing another instance of interrupted syntax – in which *hinneh* anticipates the rhetorical question of the parallel half-line, thus yielding the sense:

> If it is a matter of strength, he is mighty!
> And if a matter of justice – behold, who will summon him?![44]

Once again the reason may have been to balance the half-lines.[45]

These examples may serve to illustrate the many problems facing the translator of ancient Hebrew poetry. They could be multiplied manyfold. Those who have struggled with these texts can fully appreciate the experience of Dr Benno Landsberger, the noted Semitist, who is reported to have said that he found biblical poetry the most difficult Semitic literature he had encountered.[46] The effort, however, is richly rewarding. Without its poetry, the Bible would be far less appealing and far less powerful in its effect. From it the believing community has received far greater stimulus, encouragement, and consolation than if all had been written in prose. Without it the religious imagination, the language of prayer and praise, and even our understanding of the ways, emotions, motives, and purposes of God would be greatly impoverished. If the NIV rendering (whatever its limitations and defects) of the poetic in the Bible succeeds in wooing readers to a fuller enjoyment and appropriation of these spiritual riches, the labours of the translators will be sufficiently rewarded.

NOTES

1 Having chosen to employ the poetic format, it was no doubt a matter of course that the committees would apply it to Job, Psalms, Proverbs, Song of Songs, Lamentations and those passages in the narrative books that are readily identified as songs (Exod 15:1–18; Deut 32:1–43; Judg 5:2–31; 1 Sam 2:1–10; 2 Sam 1:19–27; 22:2–51; 23:1–7; 1 Chron 16:8–36; Hab 3:2–19; Luke 1: 46–55, 68–79). Surprisingly, however, though the blessings of Noah (Gen 9:25–7), Isaac (Gen 27:27–9, 39–40), Jacob (Gen 49:2–27), and Moses (Deut 33:2 –29), the prayers of Hezekiah (Isa 38:10–20) and Jonah (Jonah 2:2–9), and the oracles of Balaam (Num 23:7–10, 18–24; 24:3–9, 15–24) were also lined as poetry, the same was not done with the extensive poetic materials in the Latter Prophets. In the 'Preface' to the Old Testament the editors tell us that the language of the prophets, 'although frequently marked by parallelism is, except in purely lyrical passages, rather of the nature of lofty and impassioned prose'. But that judgment seems not to have been shared by the committees responsible for the New Testament, for there we find the quotations from the prophets lined as poetry.

2 Most notably, with respect to the Latter Prophets.

3 *De Sacra Poesi Hebraeorum*, 1753 (2nd edn, 1763).

4 Although hailed as the 'discoverer' of parallelism, Lowth's achievement was rather that of a judicious selection of features from earlier researches together with a cogent synthesis, coupled with extensive illustrations. For a convenient survey of Lowth's precursors as well as the long history of failed attempts to find the key to biblical prosody, see now James L. Kugel, *The Idea of Biblical Poetry: Parallelism and its History* (New Haven and London: Yale University Press, 1981), pp. 135–286.

5 Features it shares with other ancient Near Eastern poetic traditions, such as Sumerian, Ugaritic, Akkadian, Aramaic, and Egyptian.

6 In fact, Lowth drew heavily on the prophets, especially Isaiah, for his illustrations.

7 *Grundzüge des Rhythmus, des Vers- und Strophenbaues in der hebräischen Poesie* (1875); *Leitfaden der Metrik der hebräischen Poesie* (1887).

8 'Das hebräische Klagelied', *Zeitschrift für die alttestamentliche Wissenschaft* (1882), 1–52; 'Zum hebräischen Klagelied', *Zeitschrift für die alttestamentliche Wissenschaft* (1891), 234–47; (1892), 31–7; 261–75.

9 *Metrische Studien*, I, 1901; II, 1904–5; III, 1907.

10 *The Forms of Hebrew Poetry*, 1915; reprinted with a 'Prolegomenon' by David Noel Freedman (New York: KTAV), 1972.

11 The chief proponent of this method is D. N. Freedman, who in a series of studies has attempted to demonstrate its cogency (see now his 'Prolegomenon' to the recent reprint of Gray's *The Forms of Hebrew*

Poetry: pp. vii–lvi). His thesis is succinctly stated on p. xxxii: 'Without denying either the importance of stressed syllables for determining rhythm, or the possible application of a more precise quantitative system to Hebrew verse, we are persuaded that unstressed syllables played a role in Hebrew poetry along with stressed syllables, and that counting the total number of syllables in lines and larger units produces a more reliable picture of the metrical structure than any other procedure now in use.' Freedman's proposal has subsequently been carried out in detail by D. K. Stuart, *Studies in Early Hebrew Meter*, Harvard Semitic Monograph Series 13 (Missoula: Scholars Press, 1976) – too late for the NIV translators to assess. Appearing too late also were the detailed studies by Michael O'Connor, who proposes a system of syntactical rather than metrical restraints (*Hebrew Verse Structure*; Winona Lake: Eisenbrauns, 1980), and the more iconoclastic work of James L. Kugel (*The Idea of Biblical Poetry*, 1981).

12 See n. 10.

13 Which he called 'formal parallelism' or 'merely rhythmical parallelism' (the latter term being taken over from De Wette).

14 All the illustrations here are from Gray's own examples.

15 *The Forms of Hebrew Poetry*, p. 186. His judicious discussion covers only twelve pages (186–97).

16 Ibid., p. 192.

17 Ibid.

18 'Hebrew Poetic Form: The English Tradition', *Supplement to Vetus Testamentum*, 1 (1953), 132.

19 Those with one-line introductions only are : Pss 18; 73; 75; 97; 115; 147; 149. Those with one-line conclusions only are: 1; 3; 7; 11; 19; 20; 21, 25; 32; 55; 61; 84; 93; 125; 128; 131; 134; 145.

20 The words are Gray's, but Robinson says much the same: In such cases 'we must assume that we have merely verse paragraphs, which [. . .] are not part of the formal structure'.

21 'The Psalms: Style-Figures and Structure', *Oudtestamentische Studiën* 13 (1963): 43–76.

22 Ibid., p. 75. In his commentary he further observed that the psalm is composed entirely of couplets (*De Psalmen*, Korte Verklaring der heilige Schrift: Eerste Deel, Psalmen 1–41 [Kampen: J. H. Kok, 1962], p. 129).

23 'The Psalms: Style-Figures and Structure', pp. 50–1.

24 *De Psalmen*: Tweede Deel, Psalmen 42–60 (Kampen: J. H. Kok, n.d.), pp. 31–3. This further refinement of the analysis had already been made by the NIV translators, which accounts for the stanza divisions in the NIV text.

25 That the author deliberately chose to develop his main theme in just seven lines can hardly be doubted. The number seven symbolised completeness for peoples throughout the ancient Near East (as did

the numbers three, four, and ten, though these were employed for their symbolic value less frequently). Moreover, the author of this psalm gives clear evidence that he was consciously evoking the symbolic values of numbers. Seven times in the hymn he sounds 'the voice of the LORD' (referring to thunder – the seven thunders of God?) and he expressly refers to Yahweh ('the LORD') four times in the introduction, ten times in the main body, and four times in the conclusion.

26 Each stanza contains 74 syllables, as pointed out by D. N. Freedman a number of years ago (noted by M. Dahood [*Psalms III*, The Anchor Bible (Garden City, NY: Doubleday 1970), p. 113], without documentation).

27 The main attempts to account for the sequences of this hymn by appeal to Genesis 1 or the Egyptian Hymn to Aton need to be reconsidered in light of the architectonics of the psalm.

28 If it be objected that the direct quotation begun in Ps 132: 14 continues to v. 18, it need only be pointed out that the parallel of v. 16 to v. 9 clearly marks it as the close of its stanza. And this is confirmed by the thematic shift in v. 17 to Yahweh's promise concerning David.

29 Ps 77: 20 clearly continues and completes the theme of vv. 13–15.

30 Many attempts have been made to unravel the design of this passage, but only the recognition of interrupted syntax as a deliberate poetic device leads to any convincing explanation.

31 The structural balance between these may be greater than is evident from the NIV. Amos 5: 2–3 contain four poetic lines on the theme (with the introduction to v. 3 being clearly an anacrusis), and many would scan the extended introduction to v. 16 as a poetic line, resulting in another four-line stanza at the conclusion.

32 There may be others; for example, Pss 6:6a; 21:7; 71:14; 74:12; 82:5a (then 5bc would be read as the first line of the next stanza).

33 In Hebrew, both Pss 42:1 and 43:1 have two poetic lines; thus both the first and third stanzas are eight lines long.

34   (But I said,) 'I waste away, I waste away!
                    Woe to me!
            The treacherous betray!
                    With treachery the treacherous betray!'
            Terror and pit and snare
                    (await you, O people of the earth.)
            (Whoever flees at the sound of) terror
                    (will fall into a) pit;
            (whoever climbs out of the) pit
                    (will be caught in a) snare.

35 The same two verbs are brought effectively together to begin and end a half-line in Ps 34:2:

yishme'u 'anawim weyiśmaḥu.
Let-hear   the-afflicted   and-rejoice.

36 As a deliberate structural feature, it may be observed that the 'come and listen' that initiates the final stanza balances the 'come and see' (v. 5) that begins the first stanza following the exordium (vv. 1–4).

37 The same transposition is found in virtually all modern versions.

38 Such interruption within a poetic line is not unlike the interruption of syntactical sequences within stanzas already noted.

39 J. J. Stewart Perowne, *The Book of Psalms* (Grand Rapids: Zondervan, 1976 [2 vols in one; a reprint of the fourth edition, 1878]), pp. 132–3.

40 This interpretation appears to be supported by the most natural reading of *leyod'ay* ('concerning those who acknowledge me').

41 *Jeremiah*, The Anchor Bible (Garden City, NY: Doubleday, 1965), p. 29. To this bald statement he adds, '. . . but proposed emendations are all conjectural.'

42 Quite conceivably there were good poetic reasons for its unusual placement here. As it stands it helps to balance the first half-line with the second (8 syllables with 8 syllables), whereas to have reserved it for the following line would have tended to throw that line into imbalance. Furthermore, it does stand in the normal syntactical position, except for the inserted echoing parallelism of the imperative clause 'publish to Jerusalem'.

  Interestingly, the Hebrew idiom here is the same as that in Ps 87:4, namely, *zakar* (Hiphil) *hinneh*.

43 Usually emended to *hinnehu* ('behold him') or *hu* ('he [is]'). See, for example, Marvin H. Pope, *Job*, The Anchor Bible (Garden City, NY: Doubleday, 1965), p. 71; Robert Gordis, *The Book of Job* (New York: The Jewish Theological Seminary of America, 1978), p. 107.

44 If anyone objects that nowhere else does *hinneh* introduce an interrogative clause, let him take note of two other singular instances in the uses of *hinneh*: (1) with *mah* in Ps 133:1, and (2) with *'asher* in Eccl 5:17. Moreover, it is not to be overlooked that in the present passage the question is *rhetorical*.

45 See n. 42.

46 For this we have the word of M. Dahood (*Psalms III*, The Anchor Bible), p. xxv.

7 TRANSLATION PROBLEMS IN PSALMS 2 AND 4

Bruce Waltke

INTRODUCTION

A biblical translator faces at least seven kinds of exegetical problems: (1) textual (What is the text?), (2) lexical (What does the Hebrew word mean in its historical context?), (3) grammatical (What is the value of the Hebrew grammatical form? and/or What is the syntax of the clause[s]?), (4) historical (What did this text mean to its original audience?), (5) figurative (Is the poet using a figure of speech? If so, what does it mean?), (6) poetic (How should the Hebrew lines of poetry and its strophes be scanned and analysed?), and (7) theological (What does the text mean in the light of the full canon of Scripture?). Having answered these exegetical questions, he then faces the problem of how to translate his resolutions of them accurately, economically, with the same emotional dynamic, and clearly for his target audience.

In this chapter I aim to give the reader insight into how and why the translators of the New International Version (NIV) addressed textual, lexical, grammatical, figurative and theological problems in Psalms 2 and 4 in comparison to and contrast with the KJV (King James Version) and five modern versions: the RSV (Revised Standard Version), JB (Jerusalem Bible), NAB (New American Bible), NASB (New American Standard Bible and NEB (New English Bible). I omitted historical problems and poetic problems because the former are entailed in part in some of the other kinds of problems, and the latter for lack of space.

TEXTUAL PROBLEMS

With a high view of the text's inspiration by one Author, the NIV translators sought to harmonise the Old Testament (OT) with the New Testament (NT) as much as possible (where the textual and lexical evidence would allow for it).

The writers of the NT often cite in one way or another the Septuagint (LXX), the Greek translation of the OT. Occasionally the Hebrew text behind the LXX differed from the received Hebrew text, known as the Masoretic Text (MT).[1] In these cases the NIV, in contrast to some of the other translations, sometimes opted for the LXX in preference to the MT.

For example, in Psalm 2:9 the MT reads *tero'em* ('You will break them'), but the LXX reads *poimaneis autous* ('You will rule them'), probably vocalising the Hebrew consonants *tr'm* as *tir'em*.[2] The overall superiority of the Masoretic tradition[3] and the parallel *tenappeṣem* ('you will dash them to pieces') favour the MT. Nevertheless, the NIV (contra the KJV, RSV, NAB, JB, NASB, and NEB, but cf. the NAB) harmonised the text with such NT passages as Revelation 2:27; 12:5; 19:15.

In cases where the MT and LXX differ, and the LXX is not cited in the NT, the translators normally follow the MT.

For example, the LXX reads in Psalm 2:6: *Ego de katestathen basileus hup' autou epi Sion oros to hagion autou* ('but I have been made king by him on Zion, his holy hill'), presumably reading *wa'ᵃni nissakti malko 'al-ṣiyyon har-qodsho* instead of *wa'ᵃni nasakti malki 'al-ṣiyyon har-qodshi* ('I have installed my King on Zion, my holy hill'). Here the NIV (with all the versions cited above) follows the MT because it is the more difficult reading: the antecedent of 'I' in verse 6 is YHWH; in verse 7 it is the King. The LXX smooths away this difficulty of the poet changing speakers – using the same pronoun, without formally telling his audience what he is doing – by making the King the speaker in both verses.

LEXICAL PROBLEMS

The NIV harmonises the Testaments in other exegetical concerns as well. For example, in Psalm 4:4 it renders *rigzu wᵉ'al-teḥᵉṭa'u* by 'In your anger do not sin'. The translation of *rigzu* by 'In your anger' is problematic both lexically and grammatically.

The verb *rgz* means 'to shake/to quake/to tremble in trauma'. The subject may 'tremble' out of fear, anger, or an unknown emotional disturbance.

Mostly (about fifteen times) the quaking is caused by fear. The whole creation 'shakes' before God when in his anger he brings victory to his elect and judgment upon his enemies: the ground (1 Sam 14:15), the mountains (2 Sam 22:8 [= Ps 18:8]; Isa 5:25), the earth/land (Joel 2:10; Amos 8:8; Ps 77:18), and the depths of the sea (Ps 77:16) all quake in fear before him. (The earth is also said to tremble beneath four social inequities, Prov 30:21.) So also men shake and tremble in fear before impending catastrophe due to God's anger (Exod 15:14; Deut 2:25; Isa 32:11; 64:2; Jer 33:9; Joel 2:1; Mic 7:17; Hab 3:7; Ps 99:1; cf. Hab 3:16).

The exact nature of the emotional disturbance associated with the quaking is not clear in four passages: Genesis 45:24; 2 Samuel 7:10; 18:33; Isaiah 14:9. Three times (Isa 28:21; Ezek 16:43 – with the preposition *l*; Prov 29:9) the subjects shake in anger.

The dominant use of the verb, namely, 'to tremble in fear', suits Psalm 4 better than 'to tremble in anger'. With seven imperatives – 'know' (verse 3), 'tremble', 'do not sin', 'search your hearts', 'be silent' (verse 4), 'offer right sacrifices', and 'trust' (verse 5) – the king reproves feckless apostates for deserting him and the Lord in favour of false gods. Their apostasy tarnishes the lustre of his rule (verse 2). It seems more apposite in such a context for the king to command the apostates to tremble in fear before God than to tremble in anger against him or their circumstances.

The interpretation 'to tremble in fear' is further sustained by the immediate context. 'Tremble' and 'and (so) do not sin' (verse 4a) are parallel to 'search your hearts' and 'and (so) be silent' (*dmm*) (verse 4b).

The verb *dmm* ('be silent') displays its basic meaning when used of the sun (Josh 10:12–13), of men (1 Sam 14:9), of the sword (Jer 47:6), of churning bowels (Job 30:27), and of speech and other noises (Ezek 24:17; Pss 30:12; 35:15; Job 29:29). Sometimes, however, the silence is a metonymy, that is, it may be the result of destruction and death (Jer 8:14; 48:2; Ps 31:18), or the accompaniment of grief (like English 'numb with grief') (Lev 10:3 [?]; Isa 23:2; Amos 5:13 [?]; Lam 2:10; 3:28) or of fear and terror (cf. English 'struck dumb') (Exod 15:16; Job 31:34). (With the phrase *lyhwh*, 'before the LORD', it means to have faith in him [Pss 37:7; 62:5].)

Although the argument is circular – a common problem that bedevils translators – the meaning 'silent in fear' offers a good parallel to the expected meaning of *rgz* ('tremble in fear'). Fear often produces both quaking in the bones and silence of speech at one and the same time.

According to verse 4a trembling in fear will preclude the apostates from forming a conspiracy against God and his king, and according to verse 4b this fear, which will quell the rebellion, will come from searching their hearts upon their beds. In a group they are more inclined to think and act rashly and hypocritically. Off the stage of the public arena, and in the solitude and privacy of their own beds, God has a better opportunity to speak to them clearly through their consciences and convince them of moral truths expressed in the other imperatives (verse 3, and especially verse 5, 'trust in the LORD').

The Greek translators, however, opted for the rarer meaning of *rgz* and rendered it by *Orgizesthe* ('Be angry'), and this in turn became the basis for Paul's famous imperative in Ephesians 4:26: 'Be angry and sin not.' (Delitzsch, Kirkpatrick, and others try to defend this meaning as well in Ps 4:4.) The translators of the NIV New Testament interpreted the imperative as not a true volitive but as a concessive: 'In your anger do not sin.'

The KJV interprets the verb in Psalm 4:4 according to its normal usage: 'Stand in awe.' The JB, NAB, and NASB imply this notion by their rendering 'Tremble'. The RSV, NEB and NIV opt for 'Be angry'. This preference of the NIV is based partially on the theological desire to harmonise the Testaments, as can also be seen by its rendering of the imperative as an adverbial phrase ('In your anger do not sin'), conforming the text exactly with Ephesians 4:26.

The translation of *'imru* by 'search' in the same verse illustrates another policy and practice of the NIV, namely, an appeal to comparative Semitic philology in difficult passages. Dahood[4] noted that *'mr* in certain contexts means 'to look into', the root's meaning in Akkadian, Ugaritic and Ethiopic. His suggestion in Psalm 4:4 may find support in the fact that this is the only instance where *'mr* occurs absolutely without an explicit or implicit object and is more accurate than the translation 'commune with your own hearts' (cf. the KJV, RSV, and NASB) or 'reflect' (NAB) or 'in quiet meditation' (JB).

GRAMMATICAL PROBLEMS

A comparison of the NIV's unique rendering of *hirḥabta* (Ps 4:1) by 'Give me relief' versus 'Thou hast enlarged me' (KJV) / 'Thou hast given me room' (RSV), 'Thou didst set me at large' (NEB), etc., betrays a grammatical problem and the willingness of the NIV to go along with most recent research in advanced Hebrew grammar.

At issue here is whether or not the Hebrew perfective 'tense' (also known as the 'suffix conjugation') can connote a volitive force.

121

Buttenwieser[5] defended this use of the perfective against gainsayers with the following arguments:

1. Over a century ago Ewald and Boettcher recognised its existence.

2. Its use is universally recognised in several of the cognate Semitic languages: in Syriac and Aramaic of the Babylonian Talmud, Arabic, Old North Arabic, Modern Arabic, Ugaritic. According to H. L. Ginsberg 'one of the original functions of the perfect was that of an optative and precative'.

3. Its use can be predicted. The rule is: 'The precative perfect proper . . . is invariably found alternating with the imperfect or the imperative; it is by this sign that the precative perfect may unfailingly be identified.'

4. Either to uphold a view that denies this use of the Suffix Conjugation, or because they are ignorant of the use, the editors of the Hebrew Bible sometimes arbitrarily emend the text by replacing the perfect form with universally recognised volitional ones. Some exegetes, possibly for the same reasons, force some other use of the perfect form on an unyielding text. Their eisegesis is unmasked by the attempts of others to emend the same text.

5. No reason exists to deny this use of the suffix conjugation when all sides recognise that it is used in connection with the unreal moods for hypothetical situations.

This use of the perfective occurs about twenty times in the Psalms, and the NIV, in contrast to other versions, recognises its validity.

FIGURATIVE PROBLEMS

Metonymy, the use of one noun for another, is a common figure of speech in Hebrew poetry and one that challenges the translator not only to grasp the associative idea but also to decide whether or not his audience will make the connection. The NIV usually allows its readers to discover the metonymy, but sometimes it helps them out.

For example, 'Kiss the Son' (Ps 2:12) – if the Syriac,

followed by the NIV, be the correct interpretation of a difficult Hebrew form – has the associative idea in its historical culture to do homage to the king. Here the NIV, in contrast to the NASB ('Do homage to the Son'), retains the metonymy.

On the other hand, against the translators of the other versions, who either did not recognise the metonymy or refused to grant it as a possibility, the NIV helps out the reader in Psalm 4:2, translating *kazab* ('lies', as in NIV footnote) by 'false gods', its adjunctive idea in this context. The same figure is recognised in Psalm 40:4 (cf. the RSV, JB; contra the KJV, NAB, NASB, NEB) and Amos 2:4 (cf. the JB, NASB [note], NEB; contra the KJV, RSV, NAB, NASB [text]).

The use of *kazab* ('lies') with the specific connotation 'false gods' is argued convincingly by Maag[6] and Klopfenstein.[7] This translation makes it clear that the pusillanimous men around the king are tarnishing the king's glory by turning from him in the crisis, probably a drought,[8] to pagan fertility deities.

The NIV translators could have helped their readers here even more if they had rendered *bᵉne 'ish* (Ps 4:2) not by 'men' but by 'highborn men' (cf. 'men of rank', NAB; contra 'mortal men', NEB [*sic!*]) or an equivalent even as it rendered the same expression in its other two occurrences (Pss 49:2; 62:9).

The king's complaint against the feckless men of rank (Ps 4:2), his command to recognise this power in prayer (verse 3), and the petition for good (= rain; cf. Ps 85:12; Jer 5:24–5; etc.) (verse 6) take on increased cogency when it is recalled that in the theology of the ancient Near East it was supposed that the gods sent rain upon the kings they favoured and that the king was supposed to be potent in prayer.[9] Here are examples of the first dogma: Ashurbanipal, king of Assyria, boasts: 'Since the time that I sat on the throne of my father, my progenitor, Adad, has loosed his downpours, the forests have grown abundantly.' Similarly, the pharaoh brags: 'It is I who produced the grain, [because] I was beloved by the grain god. No one was hungry in my years.' Here are examples of the second dogma: It is said of the Assyrian king: 'His prayer will be well received by the god.' And it is said of the Egyptian king: 'Everything proceeding from the lips of his majesty, his father [the god] Amon causes to be realised there and then.'

THEOLOGICAL PROBLEMS

Who is the K/king, the one entitled 'A/anointed O/one' and 'S/son of God', in Psalm 2? Is he a God-man? Or merely a man? The translator's answer to that question will determine whether or not he uses capital letters (cf. Pss 44:4; 18:50). He will resolve the problem on hermeneutical and theological grounds.

The original audience probably referred this coronation liturgy to Solomon, and succeeding generations in Israel probably applied it to his successors at the time they ascended the earthly throne at Zion. Solomon and his successors were anointed and called 'son of God' (2 Sam 7:14; I Chron 22:10; 28:6–7; Ps 89:20–30). On the strictly historical level it is appropriate to translate the reference to the king with lower case (cf. the NIV footnotes to verses 2, 6–7 and the main text of the KJV, RSV, JB, NAB and NEB) because a descendant from David's own body is in view.

None of these historical kings, however, was worthy to fulfil the promise that in answer to their petitions the Lord would give them the ends of the earth as their possession (verse 8), which they would bring under their sovereignty (verse 9). When Israel's king was deposed and taken to Babylon in exile and none succeeded him to the throne, the psalm, which predicted one greater than David, became purely prophetic.

The New Testament interprets the psalm with reference to Jesus and finds a fulfilment in his resurrection (Acts 13:33; cf. Rom 1:4) and his ascension to heavenly Mount Zion (Heb 1:5; 5:5; cf. 12:22–3).

He is the Son of God with capital letters, for he was begotten by the Holy Spirit and conceived by the virgin Mary (Luke 1:35) and enjoyed glory with his Father before the world began (John 17:1–5). The KJV, RSV, NEB, NASB and NIV (contra JB and NAB) cite the psalm in the New Testament with capital letters.

Although on the historical level one might rightly opt for rendering the references to the king by lower case, on the canonical level one rightly opts for upper case, as in the NIV text. By using upper case in Psalm 2 the NIV translators expose their orthodox views not only of inspiration but also of christology.

CONCLUSION

Although none approves of all the solutions in the NIV to the exegetical problems in these two psalms, with regard to theology the NIV is matched only by the NASB in its orthodoxy, and with regard to other kinds of exegetical problems, it is unmatched in its use of proven, modern scholarship.

NOTES

1 Cf. Bruce K. Waltke, 'Textual Criticism of the Old Testament', in *Biblical Criticism* (Grand Rapids: Zondervan, 1978), pp. 47–84.
2 S. Lewis Johnson, in *The Old Testament in the New: An Argument for Biblical Inspiration* (Grand Rapids: Zondervan, 1980), pp. 17–19, follows R. H. Charles in the opinion that Greek *poimainein* may mean 'devastate' (cf. Mic 5:6; Jer 2:16; 22:22; Ps 80:14) and the parallel *patasso* 'smite' in Rev 19:15.
3 Cf. James Barr, *Comparative Philology and the Text of the Old Testament* (Oxford: Clarendon Press, 1968), pp. 207–22.

4 M. Dahood, *Biblica* 44 (1964):411. Dahood proposed this meaning also in hymnic passages even where it occurs with a direct object. This last proposal is unconvincing and should be rejected (cf. H. H. Schmid, ''mr sagen', *Theologisches Handwörterbuch zum Alten Testament* [= *THAT*], I [München: Chr. Kaiser Verlag, 1971]:211).
5 Moses Buttenwieser, *The Psalms Chronologically Treated with a New Translation* (New York: KTAV, 1969).
6 V. Maag, *Text, Wortschatz und Begriffswelt des Buches Amos* (1951), pp. 11, 81.
7 M. A. Klopfenstein, '*kzb* lügen', *THAT*, I:821; cf. also Ps 101:3; Jon 2:8; *passim*.
8 Cf. W. O. E. Oesterley, *The Psalms* (London: SPCK, 1939), pp. 131–2; Mitchell Dahood, The Anchor Bible: *Psalms I 1–50* (New York: Double-day, 1966), pp. 23–7.
9 John Eaton, *Kingship and the Psalms*, in *Studies in Biblical Theology* (Second Series, 32) (Naperville, IL: Alec R. Allenson, n.d.), pp. 29–30, 195.

8 HOW THE NIV MADE USE OF NEW LIGHT ON THE HEBREW TEXT

Larry L. Walker

The NIV translation committees kept abreast of various new ideas about Hebrew vocabulary and grammar, and any member was free to propose any new translation he thought was significant enough to deserve a hearing. Generally, the NIV translators adopted a very conservative attitude towards the text and our traditional understanding of it and the Hebrew language. Noticeable in this regard is the translation of Job, which follows extremely closely the Masoretic (traditional Hebrew) Text and shuns many modern suggested emendations.

Several of the translators had studied and taught Ugaritic, so they were familiar with the many new proposals emanating from Mitchell Dahood and his students. In some cases the new insights into vocabulary and grammar were accepted and incorporated into the translation. In most cases, for example the Psalms, the almost endless proposals by Dahood to re-edit the Masoretic Text in the light of Ugaritic and Northwest Semitic were rejected if the present understanding of the text made good sense. Of course, the older lexicons, such as BDB,[1] made no reference to Ugaritic, which did not appear in scholarly discussions until the 1930s, and mostly much later. KB[3] had included most of this new light from Ugaritic, and for English readers most of this is reflected in the translation of KB[3] by Holladay.[2] In all cases where a proposal based on Ugaritic would significantly alter our traditional understanding of the text and language, the NIV Committee on Bible Translation was not satisfied merely with references in new lexicons but would also check the Ugaritic source documents.

Although there are references to Akkadian in BDB, a wealth of knowledge of this language has accumulated since the publication of BDB. Of course, Akkadian is East Semitic and not so closely related to Hebrew as Ugaritic, which is West Semitic. In some cases, Akkadian provides significant insights into obscure Hebrew passages; in other cases, it corroborates traditional meanings of rare or uncertain Hebrew words.[3]

When we speak of the NIV's use of new light on Hebrew, we refer mainly to the post-BDB era. Most of this 'new' light has appeared, to various degrees, in the new lexicons published since BDB. Of course, BDB had already provided much new light on the language since the time of the King James Version.

The committee did not feel absolutely bound to the vocalisation of the Hebrew text since this came not from the original writers of Scripture but reflects the traditional understanding of the text by the Masoretes of the Middle Ages. Even here the NIV follows a very conservative course and rarely departs from the Masoretic Text. Factors influencing the judgment of the translators were context, the ancient versions and new light on the vocabulary or grammar from comparative Semitic linguistics. Footnotes usually reflect the reasons for the translation adopted where there is a question about the true reading of the text.

Much of the recent illumination of biblical Hebrew has already been incorporated into the newer lexicons, but some still remains only in articles in scholarly literature. In both cases, the NIV committee weighed carefully the new suggestions of various scholars and decided as a committee the soundness of new proposals affecting Bible translation.

Without question, the most significant new insights into the Hebrew language came from Ugaritic. These affected both the lexicon and grammar of biblical Hebrew. Akkadian also provided some new insights as well as confirming some older theories about word meanings.

VOCABULARY

One example of a new word suggested by Ugaritic is *ṣql*, 'grain, stalk'.[4] In 2 Kings 4:42, the Masoretic Text reads *wᵉkarmel bᵉṣiqlono*, which the AV[5] translated 'and full ears of corn in the husk thereof'. The term occurs only in this passage in the Hebrew Bible, and translators deduced the general meaning from usage and context: 'fresh *grain in the ear*' (JB, NAB), 'fresh ripe *ears of grain*' (NEB, but with a footnote indicating uncertainty). Holladay's lexicon suggested the Hebrew was 'corrupt', and BDB indicated it as 'dubious' and quoted the proposed emendation *biqla'to* ('in his wallet'), based on the Syriac and Aramaic rendering of the phrase. This idea is also reflected in the Vulgate *in pera sua*, 'in his bag'. Modern translations which reflect this tradition include RSV and NASB ('fresh ears of grain *in his sack*'), Beck ('fresh fruit *in his bread bag*'), New King James ('newly ripened grain *in his knapsack*').

In Ugaritic, the term *bṣql* is found several times in one passage (id. 2:61–7) and is repeated (lines 68–74) interchangeably with *shblt* 'ears of grain'. Although the precise meaning remains uncertain, this information from Ugaritic suggests the idea of 'grain' rather than 'sack', so the NIV translated 'heads of new grain'.

Another word whose meaning had been surmised by context but illuminated now by Ugaritic is *tishta'*, found in Isaiah 41:10,23. On the basis of its parallel with the verb *yare'* ('fear'), translators ascertained its general meaning in this context: 'afraid' (NEB), 'anxious' (JB), 'dismayed' (AV, NIV). However, the older lexicons had listed the root as *sh'h*, found in the Hithpael stem here, comparing it to such cognates as Akkadian *she'u* ('see'). On the basis of Ugaritic, the root is now (for example, Holladay) listed as *sht'* and compared to Ugaritic *tt'* ('be afraid'), which fits perfectly here. In Isaiah 41:23, the text has *nishta'ah*, but if this were a 'Lamedh He' verb, the proper vocalisation would have been *nisht^e'eh*, a fact Kimchi noted long ago. In this case, it is merely coincidence that the AV and the NIV came out with the same translation, because the NIV translators had access to this new information unknown to the AV translators. Ugaritic supports this specific rendering;[6] in fact, the same word pair is found in both Ugaritic[7] and Phoenician.[8]

Ugaritic has helped us identify a word for 'ship' in Isaiah 2:16.[9] The word *^{e}kiyyoth* is found only here in the Hebrew Bible. BDB was dubious about its meaning but Holladay correctly understood it in the light of new data on the word. The translation 'pictures' by AV is odd.[10] Versions since the RSV ('craft') reflect the new light on the word: NAB ('vessels'), NEB ('dhows of Arabia'), RSV ('beautiful craft'), TEV ('ships'). The parallelism with another word for 'ship' (*^{a}niyyoth*) plus the LXX should have provided better clues for earlier translations. The rendering of 'price' by JB is baseless. Ugaritic *ṯkt* possibly indicates it was an Egyptian loanword (*śkty*) in Canaanite.

The word in the first part of the parallel (*^{a}niyyoth*) is also found in Ugaritic (*'anyt*) and is attested in Amarna Letter 245:28 (*a-na-yi*). This word is used in connection with Tarshish probably as a means of identifying a type of vessel, as we might refer to the 'China clipper' as a type of flying aircraft. In such cases, the translator must decide whether to translate the word as a proper noun or a common noun. Most versions went with the former approach, but the NIV went with the latter ('trading ship'), but with the traditional idea of a proper noun expressed in a footnote.

Job 28:11 contains the enigmatic *mibb^{e}ki^y n^{e}haroth ḥibbesh*, which the AV translated 'He binds the floods from overflowing', apparently understanding *mibb^{e}ki^y* to be related to *bakah* ('to weep'), hence 'to flood'. In the light of Ugaritic *mbk nhrm* ('sources of the rivers'),[11] it seems tolerable not to read *ḥibbesh* ('blind') but *ḥippeś* ('explore'). This involves the interchange of labials *b*/*p* and differing with the Masoretes on the understanding of the sign for *sh* or *ś*. Since this idea is also supported by the Septuagint, Aquila, and the Vulgate, as the NIV footnote indicates, we put this idea in the text and the traditional understanding in the footnote. The new light on *mbk* did not necessitate a footnote on it.

New light on well-known passages always evoked cautious response from the NIV committee. A parade example of this is the word *ṣalmaweth* in Psalm 23:4. The root *ṣlm* is found in several Semitic languages with the meaning of 'dark, dreary, black' and is thought by many to be the root involved here instead of understanding this term to be a compound word (something virtually unknown in Hebrew) meaning 'shadow of death'. Also this view is supported by the use of 'darkness' (*hoshek*) as the parallel term in Isaiah 9:2; Psalm 107:10, 14; and Job 10:21–2. On the other hand, proponents of the traditional translation point out its use in Job 39:17, where it is parallel with 'gates of death'. Also, the LXX translators support the traditional rendering in Isaiah 9:2 (*skia thanatou*), which is continued in the Vulgate rendering *umbrae mortis*. When this passage from Isaiah is quoted in Luke 1:79, the LXX is used.

The arguments pro and con on this word left the NIV committee in a quandary. The traditional 'shadow of death' was retained in well-known Psalm 23, but a footnote represents the other possibility, 'deep darkness'. The same is done in Isaiah 9:2, but the translation 'deepest gloom' (without a footnote) is used in Psalm 107:10, 14. The Job 10:21–2 passage used 'deep shadow' in the text and gave the traditional rendering in a footnote.

Even before the discovery of Ugaritic, some translators, for one reason or another, had already reflected a new understanding of the term: Moffatt (1924) had 'glen of gloom', and Smith-Goodspeed (1929) used 'darkest valley'. Some modern translations reflected this new meaning in Psalm 23: NAB ('dark valley'), JB ('gloomy valley'), TEV ('deepest darkness'). Others keep the traditional in the text but slip the new meaning into a footnote (RSV, NASB, NIV).

Proverbs 8:22 is a passage which contains two different issues reflecting new insights from Ugaritic. First, the word traditionally rendered 'possess' (*qanah*) is attested in Ugaritic with the meaning 'create, bring forth', and the NIV reflected this new insight in its translation of Genesis 14:19,22, where the traditional translation was kept in the footnote. Similarly, in Proverbs 8:22 the new meaning was expressed in the text while the traditional rendering was retained in the footnote, thus leaving it more open to the christological view of some interpreters.[12]

Second, the word translated 'way' (*derek*) is attested in Ugaritic with a range of meaning, including 'dominion' or 'work', which can fit in this context along with the new meaning found for *qanah* ('create').[13] New light on *drk* also explains the NIV translation of Amos 8:14, where it is rendered 'god' (with a footnote, 'power'). Apparently *derek* was an epithet for the deity, 'the power of Beersheba', but other suggestions have also been made for understanding this verse.

Another well-known example of Ugaritic's illumination of the Hebrew text is found in Psalm 68:5(4), where *ba'ᵃrabot* is translated in the AV as 'upon the heavens', which must have been a guess from the context, since this word normally signifies 'desert'. This title of the Lord must be compared with the Ugaritic epithet of Baal, 'rider of the clouds (*'rpt*)'. This interchange of labials is not a serious problem since it is not without parallel within Semitic (and other) languages. In this case the NIV kept 'desert' in the footnote since this reading is not impossible here; the same was done by NASB, NEB, RSV.

In Proverbs 26:33 *kesep sigim* was translated 'silver dross' by the AV. This does not make much sense in this context, as many have noted. We would expect not dross, but something more like a coating of glaze to cover the potsherd in this proverb. We can redivide the consonants and understand the first letter as the prefixed preposition and the remaining letters as matching the Hittite word *zapzagu* ('glaze'). It is also found in Ugaritic as *spsg* and is listed in

the new Hebrew lexicon, KB[3]. The final *mem* may be the
so-called enclitic *mem* or a case of dittography since the next
word begins with *mem*.

An example of a new extension of meaning for a word
would be *magen* ('shield'), used of the king (human or
divine). The AV had already reflected this possibility in
Hosea 4:18, where they translate 'rulers' in the text and put
'shields' in the margin. The NIV at this place put 'rulers' in
the text and did not bother with a footnote, but the NIV
went beyond the AV in putting in the footnote the rendering 'sovereign' for this term in such passages as Psalms
7:10; 59:11; 84:9. (In Ps 89:18 its synonymous parallel,
'king', should be noted.) Dahood went further and put
'Suzerain' (of God) in such psalms as 3:3; 33:30; 18:30;
119:114; 144:2.[14]

PROPER NOUNS

In the matter of proper nouns in the Hebrew Bible, the NIV
was able to handle in a consistent way, in the light of our
most recent Bible knowledge, the place names and personal names that were often inconsistently treated by the
AV.[15] A case in point would be the same place name
translated two different ways by the AV: 'valley of the
giants' (Josh 15:8; 17:15; 18:16) and 'valley of the Rephaim'
(2 Sam 5:18, 22, 23; 1 Chron 11:15; 14:9; Isa 17:5). The NIV
consistently handled this as a proper noun – 'Valley of
Rephaim'.

On this same issue of references to places, the NIV was
able to make use of modern Hebrew commonly-used terms
such as Negev. The AV did not treat this word as a proper
noun but translated it as 'south' or 'south country' or
'southland'. Another example of a more modern treatment
of a place name is NIV's 'Valley of Ben Hinnom' for AV's
'valley of the son of Hinnom' in 2 Chronicles 28:3; 33:6;
Jeremiah 7:31; 19:2. Similarly, NIV had 'Hinnom Valley' for
AV's 'valley of Hinnom' in Joshua 18:16; and in Nehemiah

11:30, where AV had 'valley of Hinnom', the NIV has 'Valley of Hinnom'.

More significant, however, was the NIV's avoidance of geographical anachronisms by using 'Cush' instead of 'Ethiopia' and 'Aram' instead of 'Syria', as the AV had done.

An example of a word used in references to places and consistently mistranslated by AV was *'elon*, which it translated 'plain' as in 'the plain of Moreh' (Gen 12:6; Deut 11:30) or 'the plain of Mamre' (Gen 13:18; 14:13; 18:1). In all such cases the NIV properly translated it as 'tree(s)' (cf. also Judg 4:11; 9:6,37; 11:33; 1 Sam 10:3).

Many place names are so uncertain that translators must make a judgment with little evidence at hand. Whether in the mind of the ancient Hebrews the reference to a place in the Bible should be understood as a common noun or a proper noun may be uncertain. An example of this is found in 1 Samuel 24:2, which the AV translated with common nouns ('the rocks of the wild goats') but which the NIV expressed with proper nouns ('Crags of the Wild Goats'). Another example is found in Nehemiah 2:13, where the AV translated as a common noun ('the dragon well') but the NIV expressed as a proper noun ('Jackal Well').[16] In some cases we expressed the alternative understanding in a footnote. In 1 Kings 4:11 we put Naphoth Dor in the text and 'heights of Dor' in the footnote (cf. Josh 7:5; 10:4; 11:2; 13:5; 15:3).

In a few cases we could not be certain whether the Hebrew should be understood as a place name, personal name, or common noun (cf. Adam, Hos 6:7).

New handling of personal names reflects idiomatic Hebrew usage. Instead of Saul's father being called 'Kish, the son of Abiel' (AV), he is called 'Kish son of Abiel', for indeed his name was 'Kish ben Abiel'.

In a couple of cases of different kings with the same name(s), the NIV 'levelled' these so that the reader can follow the narrative with ease. Thus Joram is always used of the Israelite king (son of Ahab), even when the Hebrew has

Jehoram – but always with a footnote in such cases (for example, 2 Kings 1:17; 3:1). On the other hand, the Judean king Jehoram (son of Jehoshaphat) is referred to consistently as Jehoram, even when the Hebrew reads Joram (cf. 2 Kings 8:21). This same treatment was given to the names Joash (of Judah) and Jehoash (of Israel). Also the variants Nebuchadrezzar and Nebuchadnezzar were levelled to the latter.

New light from Akkadian has indicated that some proper nouns (Tartan, Rabsaris, Rab-shakeh) in the AV rendering of 2 Kings 18:17 should probably be treated as common nouns (supreme commander, chief officer, field commander). This new understanding of these words is also reflected in such translations as the JB, NEB, and NAB. A similar situation is found in Hosea 5:13, where the AV translated as a proper name ('king Jareb') an expression which the NIV took as meaning 'great king', a procedure followed by JB (with a footnote), NEB, NAB.

Occasionally, some Bible characters appear to have disappeared from the text. The name Ishtob in the AV rendering of 2 Samuel 10:6,8 becomes 'men of Tob' in the NIV translation.

In the light of our increased knowledge of Canaanite religion, modern scholars search the Hebrew text for overlooked references to this mythological background. Ugaritic has exposed the names of numerous Canaanite deities which some scholars believe are alluded to in the Hebrew Bible. A couple of these foremost deities are Yam (sea) and Mot (death). The god named Yam (sea) was not recognised in the AV, NAB, or NIV, but is reflected in some new translations: 'sea-monster/serpent' in the NEB (Job 3:8; 7:12; 9:8; 26:12), 'sea-monster' in the TEV (Job 7:12; 9:8), and 'Sea' in JB (Job 7:12; 9:8; 26:12; 28:14). The other Canaanite deity, Mot (death), is well known from the Ugaritic material, and possible biblical references are discussed in the scholarly literature but are not reflected yet in Bible translations. The NIV does not contain the divine names Yam or Mot, but it does refer to Death in Job 26:6; 28:22, where it is personified and coupled with Destruction.

The AV used the term Rahab not only as a reference to Egypt (Pss 87:4; 89:10), but also as a mythological reference (Isa 51:9). This last usage is now extended to two more passages (Job 9:13; 26:12) by the NEB, JB, TEV, NAB and NIV. All these new versions also use the term Rahab in reference to Egypt in Isaiah 30:7, where the AV translated 'proud helpers' (cf. NIV, 'cohorts of Rahab').

GRAMMAR

New light on prepositions in Hebrew has opened new doors for Bible translators. The presence of *b* in Ugaritic with the meaning 'from'[17] has led students of biblical Hebrew to see if such usage occurs in the Bible. In Deuteronomy 1:44, the Amorite destruction of Israel is described (AV) as '*in* Seir (*b^{e}se'ir*), even unto Hormah'. The NIV correctly translated '*from* Seir all the way to Hormah'. Joshua 3:16 is a good example where the geographical use of this preposition caused some confusion: the Kethiv (form in the text) had *b'dm*, and the Qere (scribal correction) had *m'dm*. The AV translated 'from Adam', and the NIV 'at Adam'. (It may be noted in passing that the Akkadian preposition *ina*, which usually means 'in', can also mean 'from' in certain contexts.) A number of contexts had already strongly implied the meaning 'from' for *b*, as in Exodus 38:8, where some bronze items were 'made from (*b*) the mirrors' of the women. In this place the AV translated 'of'. The polarity of prepositions (we wait *on* a bus) and cultural gaps between languages (we drink *from* a cup, but in some cultures they drink *in* a cup) further complicate the question of how to translate prepositions. A glance at *Young's Analytical Concordance* reveals that the AV had already used 'from' to translate such diverse prepositions as *'el* (Exod 36:22), *mul* (Lev 5:8), *'al* (Dan 6:18), *'im* (Dan 4:3,34), *qdm* (Dan 5:24), and *ben* (Gen 1:4). Basically, prepositions simply indicate the relationship of one object to another and the context plus the culture of the target language must be considered before the choice of word is picked by the translator.

In the light of Ugaritic usage, the so-called emphatic *l* has been found in various places in the Hebrew Bible. Most of these are imagined, and the *l* can be explained in other ways. The NIV reflected a possible use of this in Ecclesiastes 9:4b, with its translation of *l*ᵉ*keleb hay* as 'even a live dog'. Although this usage is listed in KB³, its presence and precise use are debated. Other alleged new grammatical insights from Ugaritic include the emphatic *k* and vocative *l*, but most of these can be explained in other ways and did not influence the NIV.

Homographs (two or more different words that look alike) in many cases have been illuminated by our increasing knowledge of the background languages of Hebrew. Often these homographs were not spelled the same in earlier Canaanite or in cognate languages. An example of this phenomenon is found in *hrsh*, which can mean 'to plough' or 'to work', and *hrsh*, meaning 'craftsman'. Although the two seem so similar in meaning, Ugaritic exposes two different roots involved: *hrt* ('to plough') and *hrsh* ('craftsman'). A different situation is found with the root *'bl*, which is now listed with two different meanings: (1) 'mourn', (2) 'dry up'. In this case comparative Semitic linguistics does not reveal two different original roots, but usage in Ugaritic and Akkadian adds light to biblical usage. Especially noteworthy in this case is the phenomenon of parallelism: *'bl* is used in synonymous parallelism with *ybsh* ('dry up') in Joel 1:10; Amos 1:2; Jeremiah 12:4; 23:10. The translators of the AV recognised only the first meaning ('mourn') for this word, but the NIV recognised and used also the second meaning ('dry up'), which fits in Isaiah 24:4,7. This meaning was also used in Jeremiah 12:4; 23:10; Amos 1:2; Joel 1:10, but with the other meaning ('mourn') kept in footnotes. The reverse was done in Isaiah 33:9 and Hosea 4:3.

FLORA AND FAUNA

Continuing new light on the flora and fauna of the Bible was utilised by the NIV. The 'spider' of Proverbs 30:28 becomes a 'lizard', and the 'snail' of Leviticus 11:30 becomes a 'skink' in the light of new information. The 'tortoise' of Leviticus 11:29 becomes a 'great lizard', and the 'turtle' of Song of Songs 2:12 is more accurately specified as '(turtle) doves'. The 'unicorn' ($r^{e'}em$) of the AV (Num 23:22; 24:8; Deut 33:17; Job 39:9,10; Pss 22:21; 29:6; 92:10; Isa 34:7) has become a 'wild ox' in the NIV, and the 'satyr' ($śa'ir$) of the AV (Isa 13:21; 34:14) has become 'wild goat' in the NIV. The 'roe/roebuck' ($ṣ^ebi$) of the AV becomes 'gazelle' in the NIV, which used 'roe(buck)/deer' to translate $yaḥmur$, which is only found in Deuteronomy 14:5 and 1 Kings 4:23 (5:3). (There are no gazelles in the AV.) Finally, although many more examples could be listed, we mention the AV 'greyhound' ($zarzir\ mothnayim$) of Proverbs 30:31, which appears in the NIV as 'strutting rooster'.

As far as flora are concerned, the famous 'rose ($ḥ^abaṣṣeleth$) of Sharon' in Song of Songs 2:1 is left in the text of the NIV but with a footnote indicating it is possibly a member of the crocus family, and in Isaiah 35:1 it is called 'crocus' in the text without a footnote. The 'juniper tree' ($rothem$) of the AV (1 Kings 19:4; Job 30:4: Ps 120:4) becomes a 'broom tree' in the NIV.

CULTURAL HISTORY

Perhaps it should be noted that our increased knowledge of cultural history as well as the language enabled the NIV to remove such anachronisms from the AV text as 'brass' and 'steel'. All these passages now have more accurately 'bronze'.

Another anachronism of the AV which the NIV removed is 'candle' (ner) in Job 8:6; 21:17; 29:3; Psalm 18:28; Proverbs 20:27; 24:20; 31:18; Jeremiah 25:10; Zephaniah 1:12. In all these passages the NIV used 'lamp', indicating the oil lamps used at that time. The famous 'candlestick' (*menorah*) becomes a 'lampstand' in the NIV.

Our increasing knowledge of cultural history also opened up the possibility of using the idea of 'impale' (in footnotes only) in Genesis 40:19,22; 41:13. This idea is put in the text itself of the NAB; the translation of the TEV, 'hang your body on a pole', is ambiguous.

An example of how our increasing knowledge of cultural history has helped us with new insights into the meaning of the Hebrew text is found in the well-known story of David and Goliath (1 Sam 17:7). The AV described Goliath's spear as having a staff like a weaver's beam, and most readers have undoubtedly concluded that this simile indicated the staff was big. Yigael Yadin,[18] however, concluded that the simile referred not to size but to appearance and shape – it had a leash or cord to enable the warrior to throw it a greater distance. Goliath's spear, with its leash for throwing, looked like the heddle-rod and its cords on a loom, according to Yadin and others. Since this unusual weapon was apparently unknown to the Israelites, they had no word for it and could only compare it to some object familiar to them. Such an aid for throwing a spear is known to have been used in the ancient Near East only in the Aegean and Egyptian spheres, and in the Bible it is mentioned only in connection with the Philistines (1 Sam 17:7; 2 Sam 21:19; 1 Chron 20:5) and Egyptians (1 Chron 11:23), all from the time of David and always describing spears of opponents. The only depiction of this weapon in Palestine was found at Tell el Farah, in the area of ancient Philistia. Most new translations leave open the point of the simile but probably imply size when they translate 'weaver's beam' (AV, NASB, NEB, JB). The NAB probably accepts Yadin's idea in its translation 'like a weaver's heddle-rod', which conjures up the idea of loops on a rod. The NIV translation 'like a weaver's rod' leaves open the nature of the simile, but avoids implying that size was the point of comparison.

THE DEAD SEA SCROLLS

The famous Dead Sea Scrolls did not provide much new insight into the Hebrew language itself, but they did affect the judgment of the NIV committee when the textual witnesses of Scripture differed. The only complete book of the Bible found among the scrolls was Isaiah, and this (or one of the other fragments of Isaiah from Qumran) caused the committee to include about eleven footnotes of references to readings from the text of Isaiah represented by the scrolls.

In most cases, the reading attested in the Dead Sea Scrolls was expressed in the NIV text itself (Isa 14:4; 15:9; 21:8; 33:8; 45:2; 49:24; 51:19; 52:5; 53:11); in one case (Isa 23:2–3) the witness from Qumran was mentioned only in the footnote. In another case (19:18), the Masoretic witness itself is split; since the minority witness of the Masoretic Text is supported by the Dead Sea Scrolls, it is preserved in the footnote. In Psalm 119:37 the reverse takes place: the reading of only two manuscripts of the Masoretic Text is supported by the Dead Sea Scrolls witness; so this is placed in the text, and the majority reading of the Masoretic Text is preserved in the footnote. In one case (53:11) involving a reference to the Dead Sea Scrolls in a footnote, the support of the Septuagint witness was uncertain, so the footnote suggested that the Greek be consulted. In Isaiah 33:8 the footnote simply states that the two Hebrew texts (Dead Sea Scrolls and Masoretic Text) are split in their witness; in this case the committee expressed the Qumran witness in the text itself and the Masoretic witness in the footnote.

In the New Testament the NIV may refer to the Dead Sea Scrolls when a quotation from the Old Testament is involved (cf. Hebrews 1:6).

NOTES

1 Francis Brown, S. R. Driver, and Charles A. Briggs, *A Hebrew and English Lexicon of the Old Testament* (New York: Oxford University Press, 1907).

2 KB[3] refers to the third edition of the lexicon prepared by Ludwig Koehler and Walter Baumgartner, which first appeared in German and English. The third edition is in German and was prepared by Walter Baumgartner, Johann Jakob Stamm, Benedict Hartman, E. Y. Kutscher and others. The first fascicle of this appeared in 1967, and William L. Holladay had access to this and additional material when he prepared his English lexicon which appeared in 1971 (*A Concise Hebrew and Aramaic Lexicon of the Old Testament* [Grand Rapids: Wm. B. Eerdmans, 1971]).

3 Harold R. (Chaim) Cohen listed numerous examples of how Akkadian confirmed or illuminated words found only once in the Hebrew Bible in his study *Biblical Hapax Legomena in the Light of Akkadian and Ugaritic* (Missoula, Montana: Scholars Press, 1978). This reflects his doctoral dissertation research under Moshe Held, his adviser at Columbia University.

4 Discussed by Dahood (*Catholic Biblical Quarterly* [CBQ] 16 [1954], p. 239; *Biblica* 47 [1966], pp. 107–8; *Ugaritic-Hebrew Philology* [1965], p. 17). Also cf. Gordon's *Ugaritic Textbook* #19.499 and KB[3], p. 984.

5 The following abbreviations are used for Bible translations: AV (King James Version, 1611), RSV (Revised Standard Version, 1952), JB (Jerusalem Bible, 1966), NAB (New American Bible, 1970), NEB (New English Bible, 1970), NASB (New American Standard Bible, 1971). On AV's use of 'corn' in 2 Kings 4:42, the reader should note this is British English 'grain', not to be confused with American 'corn' (maize).

6 Cf. W. F. Albright, *Bulletin of the American Schools of Oriental Research* [BASOR] 110 (1948):15, n. 41; H. N. Richardson, *Journal of Biblical Literature* 20 (1952):173; M. Dahood, *CBQ* 20 (1958):48–9; M. Held, *BASOR* 200 (1970):37, n. 52.

7 I*AB, II:6–7; I*AB, VI:30–1.

8 Karatepe, II:4.

9 W. F. Albright, *Festschrift Alfred Bertholet* (1950), pp. 4–5, and G. R. Driver, 'Difficult Words in the Hebrew Prophets', *Studies in Old Testament Prophecy* (1950), pp. 52–3.

10 Probably reflecting the Vulgate *et super omne quod visu pulchrum est*, 'and upon all that is fair to behold'. The Syriac also goes this direction, reflecting use of an Aramaic root *sk'* ('to look at'). For the lexicographical history of this word, see Creighton Marlowe, *The Development of Hebrew Lexicography* (Unpublished doctoral dissertation [Memphis, Tenn.: Mid-America Baptist Theological Seminary, 1985]).

11 II D, 6:47; cf. Job 38:16.
12 The majority of other new translations also express the new idea in the text, using 'created', 'formed', or 'begat' (cf. JB, NAB, RSV, TEV, LB, NEB). The LXX used *ektisen* ('created').
13 KB³ acknowledges the synonymous parallelism of *drkt//mlk* in Ugaritic but places a question mark over this meaning in the Bible. Passages suggested are Jeremiah 3:13; Hosea 10:13; Psalm 138:5b; Proverbs 31:3; Psalm 119:137. Dahood found many more in the Psalms.
14 Dahood preferred this term ('suzerain') because of its usage in 'suzerainty' treaties. He believed: 'The homographs *magen*, 'shield', and *magan*, 'suzerain, sovereign' (vocalisation based on the Punic name for 'emperor', *magon*), have been found and subsumed under *magen*, 'shield' . . .' (*Psalms I*, Anchor Bible [New York: Doubleday, 1966], p. xxxvii).
15 An example of the AV's inconsistent treatment of a special term would be 'Holy Spirit' and 'Holy Ghost', translating the same Greek.
16 The Hebrew is uncertain here, as reflected in the NIV footnote. (The AV used the term 'dragon' many times; the NIV does not contain any reference to 'dragons' in the Old Testament.)
17 *bks*, 'from a cup' (II AB, 3:16); *blḥm*, 'from the food' (S.S. 6). Cf. Dennis G. Pardee, 'The Preposition in Ugaritic', *Ugarit-Forschungen*, Band 7 (Neukirchen-Vluyn: Neukirchener Verlag, 1975), pp. 329–78. In this extensive study, Pardee presents, among other things, a good summary of the history of discussion about *b* 'from'.
18 Yigael Yadin, 'Goliath's Javelin and the *meʿnor 'oregim'*, *Palestine Exploration Quarterly* (1955), pp. 58 ff. Cf. also Edward E. Hindson, *The Philistines and the Old Testament* (Grand Rapids: Baker Book House, 1971), p. 154: and C. Knight and J. MacKenzie, *Illustrated Family Encyclopaedia of the Living Bible*, Vol. IV (Chicago: San Francisco Productions, 1967), pp. 78–9. The weapon is described in Yigael Yadin's *The Art of Warfare in Biblical Lands in the Light of Archaeological Discovery* (New York: McGraw-Hill, 1963).

9   *YHWH SABAOTH*: 'THE LORD ALMIGHTY'

Kenneth L. Barker

The translators of the NIV faced two major problems with respect to the Hebrew phrase, Yнwн *ṣeba'oth* (Sabaoth): (1) how to render Yнwн when standing alone and (2) how to translate the words when combined. These problems will be dealt with separately.

YHWH[1]

There is an almost universal consensus among scholars today that the sacred Tetragrammaton (Yнwн) is to be vocalised and pronounced Yahweh.[2] Probably the name means literally 'He is'. Some argue, somewhat philosophically or metaphysically, that it presents God as the eternally self-existent One – the absolute, unchanging God (the eternal I am – Exod 3:13–15; cf. John 8:58). To them, the name connotes the underived and independent existence of God.

Others correctly maintain that such an understanding does not go far enough. They point out that, in the Old Testament, Yahweh is used as the personal, covenant name of God, and that name is a perpetual testimony to his faithfulness to his promises. Thus in usage it conveys the thought that God is present to save, help, deliver, redeem, bless and keep covenant. In other words, God's active existence and presence are primarily in view, not his mere state of being or passive presence. He is the God who personally reveals himself in authoritative word and mighty act.

God himself identifies his name as Yahweh in Exodus 3:15; 6:3. Strictly speaking, all other 'names' are either generic terms (for example, Elohim, 'God') or appellative titles or epithets (for example, Adonai, 'Lord'). But it is not sufficient to stop with the statement that Yahweh is his name, for the word 'name' itself possesses far-reaching implications in Semitic usage. When God speaks of his 'name' as Yahweh, he means that Yahweh is his self-disclosure – his revealed character, nature, essence, or being.

In the Hebrew Bible the Jews wrote the consonants of the Tetragrammaton as YHWH, but out of reverence for the sacred name of God (or out of fear of violating Exod 20:7; Lev 24:16), they vocalised and pronounced it as Adonai or occasionally as Elohim. It is unfortunate, then, that the name was transliterated into German and ultimately into English as Jehovah (which is the way the name is represented in the American Standard Version of 1901), for this conflate form represents the vowels of Adonai superimposed on the consonants of Yahweh and it was never intended by the Jews to be read as Yehowah (or Jehovah).

The meaning assigned to Yahweh above (literally 'He is') reflects an understanding of the name as an earlier form of the Qal imperfect of the Hebrew verb *hayah*, sometimes written *hawah* (the actual original root was *hwy*). However, the form has also been analysed[3] as the Hiphil imperfect of the same verb, meaning 'He (who) causes to be', that is, 'He (who) creates' or 'He (who) brings into existence'. Exodus 3:14 ('I AM WHO I AM') may be of some assistance in deciding between these two views. In my opinion, this verse is a divine commentary on, or exposition of, the meaning of the name Yahweh (v. 15). If this is true, it obviously favours the former view, for when God speaks of himself he says, 'I AM' and when we speak of him we say, 'He is.'[4]

A problem has been imagined in Exodus 6:3 because of the words, 'by my name the LORD [Yahweh] I did not make myself known to them [that is, to the patriarchs].' Yet there are several references to Yahweh in the patriarchal narratives and earlier (for example, Gen 2:4; 4:26; 13:4; 15:7) and in names like Jochebed (Exod 6:20), apparently meaning 'The LORD (Yahweh) is glory'. Kidner points the way to one solution: 'In Ex 3:14 the divine exposition, "I am . . ." introduces and illuminates the name given in 3:15, and this remains the context for 6:3 as well [. . .] The name, in short, was first *known*, in any full sense of the word, at its first expounding.'⁵

Another approach is to let the emphasis fall on the personal, intimate, experiential sense in which the Hebrew verb for 'know' is often used (see, for example, in Exodus, 6:7; 7:17; 8:10,22; 9:14,29; 10:2; 11:7; 14:4,18; 16:6,8,12; 18:11). (The point being made here is valid whether the verb is to be translated 'I did not make myself known' or 'I was not known'.) In effect, God would be saying: 'By my name Yahweh I was not intimately and experientially known to the patriarchs. Their experience of me was largely as El Shaddai ("God Almighty"). But now, beginning with the exodus and deliverance from Egypt, I am about to reveal myself fully and personally in the experience of my covenant people Israel in that aspect of my character signified by Yahweh, that is, as the God who is ever present with his people to help and redeem them and to keep covenant with them.'⁶ This view seems to be supported by Exodus 6:4–8. In particular, the verbs in Exodus 6:6 – 'bring out', 'free', 'redeem' – stress the true significance of the name Yahweh, who is the redeemer of his people.⁷

Exodus 6:3, then, 'does not necessarily mean that the patriarchs were totally ignorant of the name Yahweh ("the LORD") but it indicates that they did not understand its full implications as the name of the One who would redeem his people [. . .] That fact could be comprehended only by the Israelites who were to experience the exodus, and by their descendants.'⁸

Although Motyer's interpretation of Exodus 6:3 is some-what different, his conclusion is similar:

> The place of the verse in the scheme of revelation, as we see it, is this: not that now for the first time the name as a sound is declared, but that now for the first time the essential signifi-cance of the name is to be made known. The patriarchs called God Yahweh, but knew Him as El Shaddai; their descendants will both call him and know Him by His name Yahweh. This is certainly the burden of Exodus vi. 6ff.[9]

To understand how 'LORD' came to be used as a trans-lation of YHWH (Yahweh), we must give some attention to the Greek word *kurios*. The latter is properly a Greek adjec-tive meaning 'having power or authority'; used as a noun, it means 'lord, sovereign, master, owner'. This is the stan-dard word for 'Lord' in the Septuagint (the ancient Greek translation of the Old Testament) and in the New Testa-ment. Essentially it was the semantic equivalent of Hebrew *Adonai* (and to some extent also of Hebrew *ba'al*), and was used in the Septuagint to translate Yahweh because the rabbis read Adonai in place of the personal, divine name. (New Testament writers applied *kurios* to Jesus as a divine title.) English Bible translators have traditionally followed the convention of rendering YHWH (Yahweh) as 'LORD' in capital letters to distinguish it from Adonai, for which small letters are used ('Lord'). The NIV translators adopted the same device.

Finally, it is instructive to observe that an abbreviated form of Yahweh is preserved in the Hebrew name Joshua and in the Greek name Jesus, both meaning 'The LORD (Yahweh) saves'.

YHWH SABAOTH

Another problem faced by the NIV translators was how to render the title 'Sabaoth' when applied to Yahweh ('the LORD').

The Preface to the NIV explains:

Because for most readers today the phrases 'the LORD of hosts' and 'God of hosts' have little meaning, this version renders them 'the LORD Almighty' and 'God Almighty'. These renderings convey the sense of the Hebrew, namely, 'he who is sovereign over all the "hosts" (powers) in heaven and on earth, especially over the "hosts" (armies) of Israel'. For readers unacquainted with Hebrew this does not make clear the distinction between *Sabaoth* ('hosts' or 'Almighty') and *Shaddai* (which can also be translated 'Almighty'), but the latter occurs infrequently and is always footnoted.

Similarly, Eichrodt concludes that Sabaoth 'does not refer to any particular "hosts," but to all bodies, multitudes, masses in general, the content of all that exists in heaven and in earth [. . .] [a] name expressive of the divine sovereignty'.[10] As 'the LORD Almighty', Yahweh is the controller of history who musters all the powers of heaven and earth to accomplish his will.[11]

Miller considers this epithet as part of the Old Testament divine warrior motif.[12] He isolates the activities of the divine warrior as salvation, judgment and kingship.[13] The messianic King was also to be a divine warrior or strong ruler ('Mighty God' in Isa 9:6; cf. Isa 10:21).

In the same vein, The *NIV Study Bible* comments on the first occurrence of 'Yahweh Sabaoth' in Scripture (1 Sam 1:3):

This is the first time in the Bible that God is designated by this title. The Hebrew for 'host(s)' can refer to (1) human armies (Ex 7:4; Ps 44:9); (2) the celestial bodies such as the sun, moon and stars (Ge 2:1; Dt 4:19; Isa 40:26); or (3) the heavenly creatures such as angels (Jos 5:14; 1Ki 22:19; Ps 148:2). The title, 'the LORD of hosts,' is perhaps best understood as a general reference to the sovereignty of God over all powers in the universe (hence the NIV rendering 'the LORD Almighty'). In the account of the establishment of kingship in Israel it became particularly appropriate as a reference to God as the God of armies – both of the heavenly army (Dt 33:2; Jos 5:14; Ps 68:17; Hab 3:8) and of the army of Israel (1Sa 17:45).[14]

Kišš, however, maintains that 'the idea of God as the God of war is secondary in the understanding of God in Israel. The primary idea of God in Israel is that God is Lord and King of the whole universe.'[15] He continues:

> According to the Old Testament view, there are different powers in the world – angels, hosts of stars, cosmic and natural powers – which are organised like an army. Above them all reigns the Lord. He is the God of gods. Thus 'Yahweh sabaoth' is, on the one hand, literally 'Lord of army hosts' but also, if we look for the abstract meaning of this formula, the 'Almighty Lord' [. . .] a 'royal' concept stressing the kingship of Yahweh.[16]

Hartley concurs with this analysis of the epithet:

> It affirms his universal rulership that encompasses every force or army, heavenly, cosmic and earthly [. . .] [Ps 24:10] clearly shows that Yahweh of hosts conveys the concept of glorious king. Yahweh is King of the world (cf. Zech 14:16) and over all the kingdoms of the earth (Isa 37:16) [. . .] Although the title has military overtones, it points directly to Yahweh's rulership over the entire universe [. . .] Special attention is given to the majestic splendor of Yahweh's rule in this title.[17]

Some illumination is gained by noting that the Greek term *pantokrator* is commonly used in the Septuagint as the semantic equivalent of Sabaoth (and of Shaddai). Michaelis defines this Greek equivalent as 'the almighty', 'the ruler of all things.'[18] The term likewise occurs in the following New Testament phrases (in each case 'Almighty' translates *pantokrator*): (1) 'the Lord Almighty' (2 Cor 6:18), (2) '(the) Lord God Almighty' (Rev 4:8; 11:17; 15:3; 16:7; 19:6; 21:22), and (3) 'God Almighty' (Rev 16:14; 19:15) – all obviously echoing 'the LORD Almighty', '(the) LORD God Almighty' and 'God Almighty' in the Old Testament. Michaelis summarises:

'The reference is not so much to God's activity in creation as to His supremacy over all things.'[19]

Kišš reminds us that when Reginald Heber, Bishop of Calcutta, wrote the familiar English hymn, 'Holy, Holy, Holy, Lord God Almighty' (Isa 6:3), the words 'Lord . . . Almighty' were a translation of the phrase 'Yahweh Sabaoth'.[20]

NOTES

1 The following discussion is based primarily on my article, 'LORD', in *Wycliffe Bible Encyclopedia*, edited by C. F. Pfeiffer, H. F. Vos, and J. Rea (Chicago: Moody Press, 1975), 2:1048.

2 For a contrary position see R. Laird Harris, 'The Pronunciation of the Tetragram', in *The Law and the Prophets*, edited by John H. Skilton (Phillipsburg, NJ: Presbyterian and Reformed Publishing Co., 1974), pp. 215–24.

3 For example, by W. F. Albright, *From the Stone Age to Christianity* (Garden City, NY: Doubleday Anchor Books, 1957), pp. 15–16, 259–61; *Yahweh and the Gods of Canaan* (London: University of London, Athlone, 1968), pp. 146–9.

4 Kenneth L. Barker, general editor, *The NIV Study Bible* (Grand Rapids: Zondervan, 1985), p. 91, note on Exod 3:15 (see also pp. 278–9, note on Deut 28:58).

5 Derek Kidner, *Genesis* (London: Tyndale Press, 1967), p. 19; cf. also Edmond Jacob, *Theology of the Old Testament* (New York: Harper, 1958), pp. 48–54.

6 Cf. J. Barton Payne's statement that the Tetragrammaton 'connotes God's nearness, his concern for man, and the revelation of his redemptive covenant' in his article on *'hawah'* in *Theological Wordbook of the Old Testament*, edited by R. Laird Harris (Chicago: Moody Press, 1980), 1:212.

7 *NIV Study Bible*, p. 94, note on Exod 6:6.

8 Ibid. p. 94, note on Exod 6:3.

9 J. A. Motyer, *The Revelation of the Divine Name* (Leicester: Theological Students Fellowship, 1959), p. 16. For a valuable and generally valid treatise on the use of the divine names Yahweh and

Elohim, see Umberto Cassuto, *The Documentary Hypothesis*, translated by I. Abrahams (Jerusalem: Magnes Press, 1961), pp. 15–41.
10 Walther Eichrodt, *Theology of the Old Testament*, translated by J. A. Baker (Philadelphia: Westminster Press, 1961), 1:193–4.
11 Cf. Kenneth L. Barker, 'Zechariah', in *The Expositor's Bible Commentary*, edited by Frank E. Gaebelein (Grand Rapids: Zondervan, 1985), 7:607, 664–5.
12 Patrick D. Miller, Jr, *The Divine Warrior in Early Israel* (Cambridge: Harvard University Press, 1973), pp. 154–65.
13 Miller, *Divine Warrior*, pp. 170–5.
14 *NIV Study Bible*, p. 375, note on 1Sa 1:3.
15 Igor Kišš, ' "The Lord of Hosts" or "The Sovereign Lord of All"?' *Technical Papers for The Bible Translator* 26/1 (January 1975): 102.
16 Kišš, 'Lord of Hosts', p. 103.
17 John E. Hartley, '*ṣaba'* ', in *Theological Wordbook of the Old Testament*, edited by R. Laird Harris (Chicago: Moody Press, 1980), 2:750–1.
18 Wilhelm Michaelis, '*pantokrator*', in *Theological Dictionary of the New Testament*, edited by Gerhard Kittel and translated and further edited by Geoffrey W. Bromiley (Grand Rapids: Eerdmans, 1966), 3:914.
19 Michaelis, '*pantokrator*', p. 915.
20 Kišš, 'Lord of Hosts', p. 106.

10 OLD TESTAMENT QUOTATIONS IN THE NEW TESTAMENT

Ronald F. Youngblood

So much of the New Testament consists of references to or quotations from the Old Testament that the so-called New Testament Christian is biblically illiterate if he knows little or nothing about the Old Testament. Reading the New Testament without knowledge of its Old Testament background is like starting to watch a two-act play at the beginning of the second act.[1] The latter experience would be supremely unsatisfying – for most of us, at least. We want to know how the play began – in its entirety, not just in its second half.

The Bible is the most dramatic literary production of all time. The preparation and promise of the Old Testament find their completion and fulfilment in the New Testament. Each half of Scripture needs the other for its fullest understanding. As Augustine put it: 'The New Testament is in the Old Testament concealed, the Old Testament is in the New Testament revealed.' Such a close relationship between the two Testaments is reason enough to warrant frequent examination of the ever-fascinating and always-important topic, 'Old Testament Quotations in the New Testament'. Each of the major elements in that title, however, is fraught with its own dangers.

151

PRELIMINARY QUESTIONS

1. *What is meant by 'New Testament'?* The so-called *Textus Receptus* ('Received Text') is the Greek form of the New Testament that underlies the KJV translation. It is now almost universally recognised that the *Textus Receptus* (TR) contains so many significant departures from the original manuscripts of the various New Testament books that it cannot be relied on as a basis for translation into other languages.[2]

An example of the effect that this has on quotations of the Old Testament in the New Testament is the way in which Luke 4:18–19 cites Isaiah 61:1–2. The phrase 'to bind up the brokenhearted' (Isa 61:1) was omitted by Jesus in the synagogue at Nazareth (Luke 4:18, NIV), as the best Greek manuscripts attest. The KJV of Luke 4:18, however, includes the phrase (translating 'to heal the brokenhearted') because it used the inferior TR as its basic manuscript. This is not to say, of course, that the TR is always wrong and that other Greek manuscripts are always right, because each variant between texts must be judged on its own merits.[3] It is simply to point out that in most cases the readings found in older manuscripts, particularly the great Greek uncials Vaticanus and Sinaiticus of the fourth century AD, are to be preferred over those found in later manuscripts, such as those that reflect the TR.

By making full use of the discipline known as textual criticism, the NIV translators attempted to employ the most accurate and original Greek text for every given New Testament passage. Such a procedure results in what is called an 'eclectic' text[4] and ensures that we are reading and studying a New Testament that is as close to the divinely-inspired original as is humanly possible.

2. *What is meant by 'Old Testament'?* It hardly needs to be stated that 'the NT reacts to the OT as the OT was experienced in the first century'.[5] But our present knowledge leads us to believe that more than one version of the

Hebrew Old Testament was available to the first-century reader who 'experienced' it. In addition, one or more Greek translations of the Hebrew Old Testament were circulating at that time, and Aramaic Targums ('translations', 'paraphrases', 'interpretations') – whether written or oral – were also current.[6] It is to be expected, then, that the New Testament writers would quote sometimes from one Old Testament version or translation, sometimes from another.[7] In every case, however, we can be sure that the inspired author quoted from or alluded to a version that did not distort the truth being asserted.

3. *What is meant by 'quotations'?* Roger Nicole reminds us that the New Testament writers did not have the same rules for quoting that we take for granted today. They neither had nor used quotation marks, ellipsis marks, brackets, or footnote references.[8] They were therefore unable to indicate readily where quotations began and ended, whether omissions occurred in their citations, whether editorial comments were being inserted or intercalated, whether more than one Old Testament passage was being quoted, etc.

In addition, 'quotations' should be understood to include allusions and paraphrases, since the NT writers often quoted from memory and therefore with greater or lesser degrees of freedom.[9] The minds of the New Testament authors were so saturated with Old Testament texts and teachings that they referred to the Old Testament in a variety of ways – now quoting precisely, now alluding to this or that passage, now paraphrasing – but never deviating from its life-transforming message.

THE QUOTATIONS THEMSELVES

1. *How many quotations are there?* Unanimity on the question of statistics is notably lacking. New Testament verses or passages introduced by a formula designating that what

follows is indeed an Old Testament quotation number 224 according to Nicole,[10] 239 according to Shires.[11] If we add to these the Old Testament citations that are not formally introduced but are nevertheless clearly intended as quotations the number is 255,[12] 'at least 295',[13] etc. (According to my own count, in the NIV there are 296 New Testament footnote references to Old Testament citations.)

If we include allusions the total rises dramatically, with tallies ranging from 442[14] to 4,105.[15] But since 'the gradation from quotation to allusion is so imperceptible that it is almost impossible to draw any certain line',[16] it is perhaps best to content ourselves with round numbers and rough estimates. S. Lewis Johnson summarises: 'There are over three hundred explicit quotations of the Old Testament in the New, and there are literally thousands of allusions.'[17] Nicole is thus able to assert that 'more than 10 per cent of the New Testament text is made up of citations or direct allusions to the Old Testament'.[18]

2. *What New Testament books quote the Old Testament, and what Old Testament books are quoted in the New Testament?* The New Testament authors were by no means the first to quote from the Old Testament. In fact, a later Old Testament author sometimes quoted from or alluded to one or more earlier Old Testament authors. Wenham points out:

> We have an instance of a later prophet quoting an earlier prophet in Daniel 9:2, where Jeremiah is quoted; references to the former prophets collectively by Zechariah (1:4–6; 7:7,12); and an instance of earlier prophets being quoted as authoritative by the elders of the land in Jeremiah 26:17 [sic].[19]

The Daniel and Zechariah references noted here are not footnoted in the NIV since it was not our normal policy to footnote general allusions. But the Jeremiah 26:18 reference, which cites Micah 3:12, is duly footnoted.

The Old Testament quotes and/or alludes to itself far

more than we usually realise. The NIV footnotes call attention to the following additional citations: Gen 50:25 in Exod 13:19; Deut 1:36 in Josh 14:9; 1 Kings 21:19 in 2 Kings 9:26; 1 Kings 21:23[20] in 2 Kings 9:36; Deut 24:16 in 2 Kings 14:6;[21] 2 Kings 10:30 in 15:12; Exod 20:4–5 in 2 Kings 17:12; 1 Kings 8:29 in 2 Kings 23:27; Deut 24:16 in 2 Chron 25:4; Lev 23:37–40 in Neh 8:15; Deut 15:12 in Jer 34:14; 1 Sam 5:5 in Zeph 1:9. An example of an important allusion not foot-noted by the NIV is Exod 20:25 in Josh 8:31.

It is generally agreed that the New Testament never quotes from the Apocrypha, though some have detected Apocryphal allusions here and there. Jude 14 quotes the Pseudepigraphal 1 Enoch (also known as Ethiopic Enoch) 1:9. Such quotations and allusions do not confer canonical status on the Apocrypha and Pseudepigrapha, however, any more than Paul's quotation of Aratus in Acts 17:28, Menander in 1 Corinthians 15:33, or Epimenides in Titus 1:12 turns the writings of pagan poets into inspired Scripture.[22] NIV footnote policy does not include references to non-biblical or extra-biblical sources.

As to which of the New Testament books quote from the Old Testament, the NIV footnotes omit from consideration Philippians to 2 Thessalonians, Titus, Philemon, and 1 John to Jude. Romans occupies pride of place with 58 footnotes, while Matthew and Hebrews are second and third (47 and 39 footnotes respectively). Needless to say, all of the New Testament books without exception make allusion to the Old Testament, however generally.

In this respect, the book of Revelation holds its own unique fascination. 'That museum of rough Old Testament allusions'[23] cites or refers to the Old Testament 'about 331' times, nearly a third of the total New Testament tally of 'rather over 1,020 direct quotations or verbal allusions to the Old'.[24] At the same time it is commonly asserted that, however many allusions it may have, Revelation exhibits no direct quotations at all.[25] The NIV footnotes rightly disagree, however, by specifying that Revelation 2:27; 19:15 quote Psalm 2:9 in whole or in part and that Revelation 1:13;

14:14 quote the phrase 'like a son of man' from Daniel 7:13.[26]

Of Old Testament books quoted in the New Testament it is generally agreed that Ruth, Ezra, Nehemiah, Esther, Ecclesiastes and Song of Songs are not explicitly cited. To this list some would add Lamentations,[27] others Chronicles.[28] But just as all of the New Testament books make at least general allusion to the Old Testament, so also the New Testament contains 'passages reminiscent of all Old Testament books without exception'. [29] And the Old Testament verse most frequently cited in the New Testament is Psalm 110:1.[30]

In a very few cases, no suitable Old Testament passage can be found as the source for what clearly seems to be direct citations of Scripture in the New Testament. In such instances it would seem that the New Testament writer is freely summarising Old Testament teaching and does not intend to quote – either *verbatim ac litteratim* or *ad sensum* – a specific Old Testament verse.

3. *What Old Testament versions do the New Testament authors quote?* Most of the New Testament citations of the Old Testament are from the Septuagint (LXX), the Greek translation in common use in first-century Palestine.[31] Various forms of the Hebrew text were sometimes cited as well – especially in books such as Matthew and Hebrews, which had Hebrew-Christian audiences in view.[32] A third source for New Testament quotations are the various Aramaic Targums, whether written or oral, on the Old Testament. Earlier opinions held that written Targums did not make their appearance until the second century AD or later,[33] but the discovery of a number of Aramaic documents (including Targums) among the Dead Sea Scrolls has increased the likelihood of the existence of written Aramaic Targums at a much earlier date. In any case, a more pervasive influence of such materials on the New Testament writers has become more plausible in the light of recent research.[34]

At one time it was thought that first-century Christian

missionaries may have compiled one or more books of notes on the Old Testament texts most useful to them in their evangelistic endeavours. Such a 'testimony book' then became the source of many New Testament citations.[35] Although this idea at first attracted a few adherents and has even gained a certain documentary credibility by virtue of the discovery of *testimonia* fragments among the Dead Sea Scrolls, its weaknesses outweigh its strengths and have caused it to fall into disfavour. Other related theories, while somewhat promising, have not gained the same kind of widespread consensus that sees the LXX version(s), Hebrew text(s) and Aramaic Targums as the major (if not exclusive) sources of New Testament quotations from the Old Testament.[36]

4. *Why do New Testament writers quote from the Old Testament?* The Old Testament was the Bible of first-century believers. They quoted from it as an indispensable aid to their ministry and mission, and they made primary use of the LXX – even when it disagreed with the Hebrew[37] – because it was such a widely disseminated version and could be read and understood by large numbers of people.[38]

When New Testament writers cited the Old Testament, they were often alluding not only to the specific passages quoted but also to its context, whether near or remote.[39] An excellent example is Hebrews 12:21: 'The sight was so terrifying that Moses said, "I am trembling with fear."' The NIV correctly footnotes Deuteronomy 9:19 as the closest Old Testament parallel, but the previous footnote recognises Exodus 19 as the overall contextual setting. It was to be expected that most first-century readers and hearers, steeped in the Old Testament Scriptures, would see in their mind's eye the entire context of any Old Testament verse or two brought to their attention.

Finally, New Testament writers quoted from the Old Testament because they believed that it pointed to the Messiah, whom they had come to know and love as Jesus

Christ (Luke 24:25–7, 44–9; Acts 3:17–26; 2 Cor 1:20; 3:14).
They read the Old Testament in the light of what Christ had
done for them and for the whole world – and so should
we.[40]

5. *How do New Testament writers quote from the Old Testament?* Wenham maintains:

> We have [. . .] no right to demand of believers in verbal
> inspiration that they always quote Scripture verbatim, particu-
> larly when the Scriptures are not written in the native language
> of either writer or reader. As with the word preached, we have
> a right to expect that quotations should be sufficiently accurate
> not to misrepresent the passage quoted; but, unless the
> speaker makes it clear that his quotation is meant to be ver-
> batim, we have no right to demand that it should be so. In the
> nature of the case, the modern scholarly practice of meticul-
> ously accurate citation, with the verification of all references,
> was out of the question.[41]

Given these parameters it is possible, with R. T. France,[42]
to distinguish the following five forms of Old Testament
text quoted or alluded to in the New Testament: (1) those
that agree with both LXX and Hebrew, constituting more
than half the total number;[43] (2) those that agree with one
LXX text against another; (3) those that agree with the LXX
against the Hebrew; (4) those that agree with the Hebrew
against the LXX; (5) those that differ from both LXX and
Hebrew. The latter would include citations from one or
more Aramaic Targums (oral or written), free renderings[44]
of the substance of a passage, etc.

Various combinations of passages cited from two or more
Old Testament books are not uncommon in the New Testament. A fine example is Romans 3:10–18, which, according
to the NIV footnotes there, quotes from the Psalms, Isaiah
and (perhaps) Ecclesiastes. A noteworthy variation of this
phenomenon is the so-called *ḥaraz* ('chain', 'necklace'; the
same Hebrew root is used in Song of Songs 1:10, where it is
translated 'strings of jewels'), which intersperses a series of

quotations with conjunctions, introductory formulae, and the like (see, for example, Rom 9:25–9[45] and NIV footnotes there).

When a New Testament writer quoted an Old Testament prophecy or promise, he was not necessarily saying that the Old Testament text in question was a direct prophetic prediction being fulfilled in his own time.[46] In a substantial number of cases the relationship of the Old Testament text to its New Testament citation is that of type to antitype, and the Old Testament passage is an example of what I have elsewhere called 'typological prefiguration'.[47] The New Testament writers' approach to the Old Testament was not as one-dimensional as it is often made out to be. 'The Early Church looked upon the OT as a prophecy, as a history (the book of preparation), as a promise, and as the book of prefigurations.'[48]

Typology is almost universally recognised as a legitimate hermeneutical method that can be used to clarify the relationship between the Old Testament and the New Testament.[49] 'Typology connotes two factors: a set of correspondences between objects or actions in both Testaments, and an indication that their interrelations are God-willed.'[50] As long as the first is controlled by the second – and we can be reasonably sure of that only as we rely on the insights expressed in the words of the apostolic authors of the New Testament – only then can we prevent typological method from vaporising into flights of fancy.

CONCLUSION

Jean Levie gave to his book on biblical criticism and exegesis this perceptive title: *The Bible, Word of God in Words of Men*.[51] The subtle symbiosis between divine and human authorship in Scripture is present in such a way as to give us divine truth without admixture of human error. This fact is none the less true with respect to Old Testament quotations in the New Testament than with respect to any other biblical phenomenon.[52]

At the same time, 'when the Holy Ghost in the New Testament quotes something He said in the Old, He is completely independent of all human versions. He is His own infallible interpreter.'[53] Since 'all Scripture is God-breathed', Old Testament quotations in the New Testament are – like the rest of the Bible – 'useful for teaching, rebuking, correcting and training in righteousness' (2 Tim 3:16). The NIV thus performs a useful service for its readers by setting off in quotation marks almost 300 citations of the Old Testament in the New Testament location.

NOTES

1 J. Bright, *The Authority of the Old Testament* (Nashville: Abingdon, 1967), pp. 202–3.

2 See chapters 4 and 14 of the present volume.

3 Cf. the examples given by B. F. C. Atkinson, 'The Textual Background of the Use of the Old Testament by the New', *Journal of the Transactions of the Victoria Institute* 79 (1947): 49.

4 See NIV Preface for further details; see also chapter 4 of the present volume.

5 R. E. Murphy, 'The Relationship Between the Testaments', *Catholic Biblical Quarterly* 26/3 (July 1964): 356.

6 See NIV Preface for further details; see also Atkinson, 'Textual Background', pp. 39–41, 54–5; S. L. Johnson, Jr, *The Old Testament in the New* (Grand Rapids: Zondervan, 1980), p. 54; G. L. Archer, Jr, and G. Chirichigno, *Old Testament Quotations in the New Testament* (Chicago: Moody, 1983), pp. ix, xi, xxv–xxvi; S. Davidson, *Sacred Hermeneutics* (Edinburgh: T. and T. Clark; London: Hamilton Adams, 1843), pp. 334–5; C. E. Armerding, *The Old Testament and Criticism* (Grand Rapids: Eerdmans, 1983), p. 106; R. Nicole, 'New Testament Use of the Old Testament', in *Revelation and the Bible* (ed. C. F. H. Henry; Grand Rapids: Baker, 1958), p. 142.

7 See NIV footnotes to 2 Tim 2:19; Heb 10:7.

8 Nicole, 'New Testament Use', p. 144.
9 See ibid., pp. 144–5; R. T. France, *Jesus and the Old Testament* (Downers Grove: InterVarsity, 1971), pp. 27, 259; E. E. Ellis, *Paul's Use of the Old Testament* (Grand Rapids: Eerdmans, 1957), pp. 11, 14–15; *Old Testament Quotations in the New Testament* (rev. edn; ed. R. G. Bratcher; London: United Bible Societies, 1967), p. vii; J. W. Wenham, *Christ and the Bible* (Downers Grove: InterVarsity, 1973), p. 103; Archer and Chirichigno, *Old Testament Quotations*, pp. xxviii, xxxii; H. M. Shires, *Finding the Old Testament in the New* (Philadelphia: Westminster, 1974), pp. 16–17; Atkinson, 'Textual Background', pp. 39–41.
10 Nicole, 'New Testament Use', p. 137.
11 Shires, *Finding*, p. 66.
12 Davidson, *Sacred Hermeneutics*, p. 446.
13 Nicole, 'New Testament Use', p. 137.
14 *Old Testament Quotations* (ed. Bratcher).
15 Nicole, 'New Testament Use', p. 138. Cf. also W. C. Kaiser, Jr, *The Uses of the Old Testament in the New* (Chicago: Moody, 1985), p. 2.
16 Ellis, *Paul's Use*, p. 11.
17 Johnson, *Old Testament*, p. 27.
18 Nicole, 'New Testament Use', p. 138.
19 Wenham, *Christ and the Bible*, p. 128.
20 See also NIV footnote there for a discussion of textual variants in the verse.
21 Inexplicably, the NIV reads 'sin' in Deut 24:16 but 'sins' in 2 Kings 14:6 and its parallel 2 Chron 25:4, though the Hebrew word is identical in all three passages.
22 Wenham, *Christ and the Bible*, p. 145; Davidson, *Sacred Hermeneutics*, pp. 336–7; E. A. Blum, 'Jude', in *The Expositor's Bible Commentary* (ed. F. E. Gaebelein *et al.*; Grand Rapids: Zondervan, 1981), 12:393.
23 Atkinson, 'Textual Background', p. 45.
24 According to ibid., p. 39.
25 C. H. Toy, *Quotations in the New Testament* (New York: Scribner's, 1884), p. xxxvii; R. V. G. Tasker, *The Old Testament in the New Testament* (Grand Rapids: Eerdmans, 1968), p. 146; Kaiser, *Uses*, p. 3.
26 Johnson, *Old Testament*, p. 17, agrees concerning Revelation that 'there is not one formal citation from the Old Testament in the book' but immediately goes on to say – inexplicably and obfuscatingly – that 'many of the allusions, however, are intended as citations'.
27 Wenham, *Christ and the Bible*, p. 159.
28 Nicole, 'New Testament Use', p. 138.
29 Ibid.
30 For details see Atkinson, 'Textual Background', p. 52. Several of the volumes that deal extensively with quotations of the OT in the NT include helpful indices that list, in canonical order, NT quotations as

well as OT passages cited (see, e.g., Toy, *Quotations*, pp. 283–316; Shires, *Finding*, pp. 215–51).

31 'Interestingly the quotations from the Septuagint agree mainly with the characteristically Palestinian form of the LXX, represented by MSS A, Q and Lucian' (Wenham, *Christ and the Bible*, p. 95).

32 Archer and Chirichigno, *Old Testament Quotations*, p. ix. The situation with respect to the book of Hebrews is not so clear as with Matthew, however; see, for example, Atkinson, 'Textual Background', p. 39.

33 Cf. for example, Toy, *Quotations*, pp. xiv–xv; F. F. Bruce in Atkinson, 'Textual Background', pp. 60–2.

34 See especially M. McNamara, *Targum and Testament* (Grand Rapids: Eerdmans, 1972).

35 J. R. Harris, *Testimonies* (2 vols; Cambridge University Press, 1916, 1920).

36 See further Ellis, *Paul's Use*, pp. 98–113; D. M. Smith, Jr, 'The Use of the Old Testament in the New', in *The Use of the Old Testament in the New and Other Essays* (ed. J. M. Efird; Durham: Duke University, 1972), pp. 25–30.

37 See NIV footnotes to 2 Tim 2:19; Heb 10:7; Ps 40:6.

38 Davidson, *Sacred Hermeneutics*, p. 335; Archer and Chirichigno, *Old Testament Quotations*, p. ix; Ellis, *Paul's Use*, p. 12.

39 Johnson, *Old Testament*, p. 76; C. H. Dodd, *The Old Testament in the New* (Philadelphia: Fortress, 1963), p. 20; C. Westermann, *The Old Testament and Jesus Christ* (Minneapolis: Augsburg, n.d.), pp. 12–14; S. L. Edgar, 'Respect for Context in Quotations from the Old Testament', *New Testament Studies* 9 (1962–3), pp. 55–62. Contrast R. T. Mead, 'A Dissenting Opinion about Respect for Context in Old Testament Quotations', *NTS* 10 (1963–4), pp. 279–89.

40 See, for example, B. K. Waltke, 'Is it Right to Read the New Testament into the Old?', *Christianity Today*, 2 September, 1983, p. 77; Wenham, *Christ and the Bible*, p. 107.

41 Wenham, *Christ and the Bible*, p. 92.

42 France, *Jesus*, p. 27.

43 Archer and Chirichigno, *Old Testament Quotations*, p. xxv.

44 Such free quotation need not distort the quoted author's intended meaning, of course; see, for example, Johnson, *Old Testament*, p. 11; Wenham, *Christ and the Bible*, p. 93.

45 For further examples see Ellis, *Paul's Use*, p. 186.

46 Johnson, *Old Testament*, p. 76.

47 R. Youngblood, 'A Response to "Patrick Fairbairn and Biblical Hermeneutics as Related to the Quotations of the Old Testament in the New"', in *Hermeneutics, Inerrancy, and the Bible* (ed. E. D. Radmacher and R. D. Preus, Grand Rapids: Zondervan, 1984), pp. 779–88. See also R. R. Nicole in ibid., pp. 767–76; S. L. Johnson in ibid., pp. 791–9.

48 Murphy, 'Relationship', p. 353.
49 See, for example, Johnson, *Old Testament*, p. 76; A. B. Mickelsen, *Interpreting the Bible* (Grand Rapids: Eerdmans, 1963), p. 40; Wenham, *Christ and the Bible*, pp. 99–107; W. M. Dunnett, *The Interpretation of Holy Scripture* (Nashville: Thomas Nelson, 1984), pp. 49–54).
50 Murphy, 'Relationship', p. 357.
51 London: Geoffrey Chapman, 1961.
52 See, for example, Nicole, 'New Testament Use', pp. 147–8.
53 B. B. Knopp in Atkinson, 'Textual Background', p. 66. See also similarly Nicole, 'New Testament Use', p. 148.

11   THE ONE AND ONLY SON

Richard N. Longenecker

Two matters that are joined in John's Gospel and Letters have become bones of contention among Christians and require great care on the part of translators. The first has to do with how to translate *monogenes*, which in christological contexts KJV rendered 'only begotten' and NIV expresses as 'one and only'. The second concerns the nuancing of *huios* ('son') when used of Jesus, particularly in light of the fact that Christians are commonly referred to in the New Testament as *huioi theou* ('sons of God').

The adjective *monogenes* appears in the New Testament nine times, either with its noun or as a substantive: three times in Luke, once in Hebrews, four times in John, and once in 1 John. Thus it appears only in the later writings of the New Testament and on the part of authors who seem to be most conversant with Hellenistic modes of expression. In Luke it is used of a widow's son (7:12, 'the only son of his mother'), of Jairus's daughter (8:42, 'his only daughter'), and of the son of an unnamed man in the crowd (9:38, 'he is my only child'). In Hebrews it is used of Isaac, who was *ton monogene* of Abraham (11:17). Only in John's Gospel and First Letter is it used to describe the relation of Jesus to God (John 1:14,18; 3:16,18; 1 John 4:9).[1]

The synoptic Gospels (particularly Matthew) frequently refer to Jesus as *huios theou* (for example, Matt 14:33; 16:16; 28:19; Mark 1:1; Luke 1:32,35) and to Christians as *huioi theou* (for example, Matt 5:45; Luke 6:35). And so do the letters of the New Testament (for example, 'Son of God' in

Rom 1:3,4,9; 5:10; 8:3,29,32, etc.; Heb 1:2, 8; 4:14; 5:8; etc.; 'sons of God' in Rom 8:14,19; 9:26; 2 Cor 6:18; Gal 3:26; 4:6–7). In the Johannine writings, however, the pattern is somewhat different, for there (1) *huios theou* is used with even greater frequency for Jesus (for example, John 1:49; 3:16–18,35–36; 5:19–26; 6:40; 8:35–36, etc.; 1 John 1:3,7; 2:22–24; 2 John 3,9), and (2) *huios* is reserved for Jesus alone. Whereas elsewhere in the New Testament Christians are commonly referred to as *huioi theou* ('sons of God'), in the Johannine writings they are called *tekna theou* ('children of God', John 1:12; 11:52; 1 John 3:1,2,10; 5:2) – *huios theou* being reserved for Jesus alone.

This is not to suggest that there was little difference between the sonship of Jesus and that of Christians for the synoptic evangelists, or for Paul, or for the other writers of the New Testament. They had other ways of signalling the uniqueness of Jesus's sonship *vis-à-vis* that of Christians. It is, however, to point out that John more clearly emphasises the uniqueness of Jesus's sonship in his frequent use of 'Son of God' for Jesus and his consistent use of 'children of God' for Christians. And it is to note that the Johannine formula *monogenes huios* was what the early Church – from at least Irenaeus on – found to be both illuminating and easily remembered, and that under the influence of the Latin translation *unigenitus* it became almost sacrosanct in the creeds and Christian theology as 'only begotten Son'.

The question, however, is: What does 'only begotten Son' mean? If it has to do with origin, derivation or descent, how does that square with the Son's eternality? And if uniqueness is the dominant connotation of the word, how does that relate to the Son's oneness with believers? It is in the Johannine writings that these issues are focused. And it is to these issues that all translators of the New Testament must speak – first by way of linguistic usage and conceptual backgrounds, and then in terms of the New Testament's own christological perspectives.

LINGUISTIC USAGE

The word *monogenes*, with its variants *mounogeneia* (an early feminine poetic form) and *mounogonos* (a later masculine form), occurs first in extant Greek literature in the writings of the eighth-century BC poet Hesiod. Thereafter it appears in the work of such diverse authors as Parmenides, Aeschylus, Plato, Herodotus, Apollonius Rhodius and Antoninus Liberalis, as well as in the Orphic Hymns. It also appears in a number of Greek papyri and inscriptions.[2] Literally, *monogenes* means 'sole descent' or 'the only child of one's parents'. It is a stronger term than the simple *monos*, for it denotes that the parents have never had more than this one child. This is one way in which it was used by Hesiod (*Works and Days*, 376; *Theogony*, 426), Plato (*Critias*, 113d), Herodotus (*History*, 7.221), and Antoninus Liberalis (*Mythographi Graeci*, ed. E. Martini, II [1896], 32.1).

The word, however, was also used by Hesiod (*Works and Days*, 374; *Theogony*, 448) and the writers of the Orphic Hymns (29:2; 32:1; 40:16) in the sense of 'peerless', 'matchless', 'unique', 'of singular importance', or 'the only one of its kind', which ideas have more to do with quality than derivation or descent. The sixth-fifth-century BC philosopher Parmenides spoke of Being as 'ungenerated [*ageneton*], imperishable, whole, unique [*mounogenes*], and without end' (Frag. 8.3–4), thereby ignoring – particularly in parallel with *ageneton* – any idea of generation in the word as might be found etymologically in *genos*. In the early fifth century, Aeschylus has Queen Clytaemnestra, in mocking welcome, hail her husband King Agamemnon as *monogenes teknon patri* (*Agamemnon*, 898) – which must mean something like 'the favoured or chosen child of his father' Atreus, and not the only child of Atreus, since Menelaus was also a son of Atreus and Agamemnon's brother. Plato, in arguing that the Creator (*ho poion kosmous*) did not make two or more heavens but one heaven only, strengthens his insistence on 'one' by writing *heis hode monogenes ouranos* (*Timaeus*, 31b). And in the magical papyri, the term *monogenes* often appears as part of the title of the deity invoked: *theos, ho monogenes* or *ho heis monogenes*, which translates as 'God, the Incomparable One' or 'The One Incomparable' – though, as is evident from the context, not a god who is alone of its kind.

Likewise the LXX and various Jewish writings in Greek use *monogenes* in more than one way. The LXX translates *yaḥid* in Judges 11:34 by *monogenes*, and so identifies Jephthah's daughter as Jephthah's only child. And this stress on 'sole descent' or 'the only child of one's parents' is uppermost in the use of the word for Raquel's daughter Sarah in Tobit 3:15; 6:10; 8:16 and for Tobit's son Tobias in Tobit 6:14 and 8:16 (cf. Pseudo-Philo, 39:11). But the idea of sole descent gave rise to more general meanings for the term as well, depending on the context. So in Psalms 25:16 and 68:6 (LXX) the idea of 'the only one' is nuanced to mean 'desolate' or 'solitary' or 'all alone' (NIV 'lonely'); while in Psalms 22:20 and 35:17 (LXX) *ten monogene mou* is set in parallel fashion to *ten psuchen mou* to signify one's 'priceless and irreplaceable' life (NIV 'my precious life').

Further, in Genesis 22:2, 12, 16 and Jubilees 18:2,11,15 (possibly also *Antiq.*, 1.222), *monogenes* is used of Isaac in the sense of Abraham's 'favoured,' 'chosen', or 'unique' son, *vis-à-vis* Ishmael. It is also used in *Antiquities*, 20.20 in this manner of Monobazus' son Izates (*vis-à-vis* Monobazus' many other children), in 1 Baruch 4:16 of a widow's son (*vis-à-vis* anything else). In Psalms of Solomon 18:4 and Ezra 6:58 Israel is referred to as both God's *prototokos* and God's *monogenes* (cf. also Pseudo-Philo, 39:11), which hints at something of an overlap of meaning between the two terms. And since the LXX also renders *yaḥid* by *agapetos* (Gen 22:2,12,16: Prov 4:3; Jer 6:26: Amos 8:10; Zech 12:10), there is the suggestion that *monogenes* may also carry the idea of 'beloved' or 'best-loved'.[3]

Writing about the same time as the Fourth Evangelist (that is, AD 95–96), Clement of Rome spoke of the Phoenix, that mysterious bird of the East, as *monogenes* – that is, as 'unique' or 'the only one of its kind':

Let us consider the marvellous sign which is seen in the regions of the east, that is, in the regions about Arabia. There is a bird, which is named the Phoenix. This, being the only one of its kind [*touto monogenes huparchon*], lives for 500 years; and when it reaches the time of its dissolution that it should die, it makes for itself a coffin of frankincense and myrrh and other spices, into which in the fulness of time it enters and then dies. But as the flesh rots, a certain worm is engendered, which is nurtured from the moisture of the dead creature, and puts forth wings. Then when it has grown lusty, it takes up that coffin where are the bones of its parent, and carrying them, it journeys from the country of Arabia even unto Egypt, to the place called the City of the Sun – and in full daylight and in the sight of all, it flies to the altar of the Sun and lays them on it. And this done, it then returns. So the priests examine the registers of the times, and they find that it has come when the five hundredth year is completed (1 Clement 25).[4]

The only second-century Christian writings to use *monogenes* of Christ are Justin Martyr's Dialogue with Trypho (105), the Martyrdom of Polycarp (20.2), and the apology called the Epistle to Dionetus (10.2). Martyrdom of Polycarp 20.2, for example, is a doxology: 'Now unto him who is able to bring us all by his grace and bounty unto his eternal kingdom, through his one and only Son Jesus Christ [*dia paidos autou, tou monogenous Iesou Christou*], be glory, honour, power, and greatness for ever.' But while these second-century ascriptions presuppose a recognised semantic range of meaning for the word *monogenes*, they do not aid us in determining what that meaning was. For this we must turn back to the New Testament itself and study the epithet in light of then current usage and the New Testament's own christological perspectives.

CONCEPTUAL BACKGROUNDS

In the Old Testament and the literature of Second Temple Judaism, the Jewish people are often spoken of in terms of sonship (for example, Exod 4:22–3; Isa 1:2; 30:1; 63:16; Jer 3:19; Hos 11:1; Ecclus 4:10; Pss Sol. 13:9; 17:27–30; 18:4; Jub 1:24–5). They were the sons of God in a manner not true of any other nation or people because of their election by God and God's establishment of his covenant with them. In that relationship, God pledged himself to them and they were expected to respond in loving obedience. Together with this corporate understanding of sonship, there also exists in the Old Testament the concept of the king, who was God's anointed representative, as God's son (for example, 2 Sam 7:14; Pss 2:7; 80:26–7), so that it may be said that in first-century Judaism ideas of Israel as God's son and the anointed king as God's son existed side by side. In addition, we now know from the Dead Sea scroll 4QFlorilegium in its comment on the words 'I will be his father, and he will be my son' of 2 Samuel 7:14a – 'The "he" in question is the Scion of David who will reign in Zion in the Last Days, alongside the Expounder of the Law' – that the category of sonship was beginning to be extended to the Davidic Messiah in at least one Jewish group prior to the advent of Christianity.[5] In all these cases, whether corporate or individually understood, 'Son of God' must be seen as an epithet to designate one whose relationship with God can be characterised as one of loving obedience.

It is in the light of this conceptual background that the title as applied to Jesus must initially be seen. 'Son of God' cannot be understood simply in terms of popular religious notions that were circulating in the Greek world.[6] Contrary to the assumption of an origin in Hellenism, it is in the literature of the Jewish mission of the early church that the ascriptions 'Son of God' and 'the Son' are most prominent, and not, it should be noted, in those canonical writings that represent the Gentile cycle of witness. It is Matthew among the synoptic evangelists who gives increased prominence to the sonship of Jesus,[7] the writer to the Hebrews who begins on this theme and continues it throughout his letter (see especially 1:1–5; 2:10–18; 4:14–16; 5:7–9), and John who makes the sonship of Jesus the high point of his christology (see especially John 20:31; 1 John 4:15; 5:5). Paul, of course, highlights the sonship of Christ, for he finds in Christ's response of loving obedience the basis for our acceptance by God (cf. Gal 4:4–7). In comparison to Matthew, Hebrews and John, however, Paul's use of 'Son of God' only three times and 'the Son' twelve times seems rather surprising.[8] Likewise, Mark and Luke unquestionably believe Jesus to be the Son of God. But when they speak in such a manner, they seem, with the possible exception of Mark 1:1, to be only repeating traditional wording. Their omission of the title in Peter's confession (Mark 8:29; Luke 9:20; cf. Matt 16:16) and in the rulers' taunt (Mark 15:30; Luke 23:35; cf. Matt 27:40,43) – together with Luke's treatment of the centurion's claim (Luke 23:47; cf. Matt 27:54; Mark 15:39) – is more likely due to a desire to downplay distinctive Jewish motifs in the Gentile mission than to an expansionist policy on Matthew's part.[9]

Probably the earliest Jewish believers, in explicating their conviction regarding Jesus as Messiah, used 'Son' and 'Son of God' as epithets for Jesus in a more functional manner to denote Jesus's unique relationship to God and his response of loving obedience to the Father's will. Just as Israel and her sons were uniquely God's own among all the people of the earth, and just as the anointed king was God's son, so Jesus as Israel's Messiah, who united in his person both the corporate ideal and descent from David and who exemplified in his life an unparalleled obedience, was the Son of God *par excellence*.

That a corporate understanding of sonship was understood to be fulfilled and heightened in Jesus is suggested by the retention in the tradition of the argument of John 10:34–6, where, by means of an *a minori ad maius* inferential approach, Jesus is presented as saying: 'Is it not written in your Law, "I have said you are gods"? If he called them "gods", to whom the word of God came – and the Scripture cannot be broken – what about the one whom the Father set apart as his very own and sent into the world? Why then do you accuse me of blasphemy because I said, "I am God's

Son''?[10] And that a fulfilment in terms of royal sonship was understood as well is indicated in the application of 2 Samuel 7:14 and Psalm 2:7 to Jesus in Acts 13:33 and in Hebrews 1:5; 5:5.[11] In Jesus, therefore, whether or not they had ever been so united before, the corporate and royal Son-of-God motifs were brought together.

The New Testament, however, also indicates that, while originally understood primarily in functional ways to denote Jesus's unique relationship to God and his loving obedience to the Father's will, 'Son of God' very soon came to signify divine nature. Under the guidance of the Holy Spirit and as forced to think more precisely because of circumstances, the Church's understanding of the person of its Lord grew, and further significance was soon seen in the title Son of God. So, it seems, while early Christian tradition spoke in primarily functional ways of Jesus as 'the Son of God' and of believers in Jesus as 'sons of God', John, whose writings reflect a more deliberate christological nuancing, prefers to reserve 'Son of God' for Jesus alone and to use 'children of God' for Christians.

CHRISTOLOGICAL PERSPECTIVES

Undoubtedly sonship meant for Jesus, first of all, all that it had come to mean in the sacred and devotional literature of the Jews: his life's purpose was to do the Father's will and to offer unto God the perfect response of loving obedience. He was, as our canonical Gospels portray him, *the* Jew standing on behalf of all his fellow Jews and *the* Man representing all men, who offered in fullest measure that loving obedience which is rightfully due to God the Father – and, therefore, he has the greatest right to the title 'Son of God'. But more is involved than this. For by the manner in which he spoke of God as his Father and of himself as God's Son, Jesus signalled a consciousness of filial relationship with God that is not just quantitatively greater than any other but also qualitatively to be distinguished from all others. His references to God as 'my Father', for example, suggest an intimacy with God that surpasses the heights of Jewish piety, for the usual manner of addressing God by Jews was to use the corporate and formal 'our Father' (as even Jesus taught his disciples to do).[12] And his frequent equation of himself with the Father (for example, Mark 2:1–12; 12:1–9; John 6:32–3; 14:8–11) highlights such a qualitative difference as well.

For the early Christians, the confession of Jesus as Messiah involved also the acclamation of Jesus as the Son of God. The titles are brought together as being roughly synonymous in a number of New Testament passages (for example, Matt 16:16; 26:63; Mark 1:1; Luke 4:41; John 11:27; 20:31; Acts 9:20–2). Indeed, as God's Anointed One, Jesus was God's Son *par excellence*, offering to the Father the response of loving obedience that is God's due. But he was also, as the early Christians came to realise more and more by the Spirit's direction, God's Son because of who he was. So Jesus's sonship came to be viewed not only in functional terms but also in ontological terms, with both understandings being depicted in the canonical writings of the apostolic Church.

It seems best, therefore, to understand in a more functional way the christological use of 'Son' and 'Son of God' where early Christian tradition is being reported (though always with the realisation that in the substrata of that tradition were theological affirmations of an ontological nature that were bursting to come to the fore), and to acknowledge a more explicit nuancing of the titles in the more avowedly theological writings. Thus in the synoptic Gospels sonship is attributed both to Jesus and to believers in a manner that is primarily functional, with that of Jesus being set off from others by the addition of the adjective *agapetos* ('beloved', 'best-loved')[13] or its variant *eklelegmenos* ('chosen');[14] whereas in John's Gospel and Letters, 'Son' and 'Son of God' are reserved for Jesus alone and the adjective *monogenes* is used to support the noun *huios*.[15]

CONCLUSION

Contemporary Greek usage allows for *monogenes* to be understood more broadly as an adjective stressing quality, rather than derivation or descent. And John's nuancing of 'Son' in his Gospel and Letters lends support to such an understanding. We must conclude, therefore, that the translation 'only begotten Son', though venerable, fails to capture adequately John's point in his use of *monogenes huios* (or, *monogenes theos* in John 1:18), particularly because it leaves open the possibility of an etymological emphasis on *genes* (the idea of generation), because it neglects then current usage for the word, and because it fails to set the determination of meaning in the context of John's avowedly heightened christological perspective. Rather, we must insist that in Johannine usage *monogenes* is an adjective connoting quality, which should be translated in a manner signalling primarily uniqueness, and that *huios* as a christological appellative in John's Gospel and Letters connotes primarily divine nature. So, to be true to John's intent, *monogenes huios* is best translated into current English as 'one and only Son' (NIV).

NOTES

1 The synoptic Gospels portray God as identifying Jesus as *ho huios mou, ho agapetos* at Jesus's baptism (Matt 3:17; Mark 1:1; Luke 3:22) and at his transfiguration (Matt 17:5; Mark 9:7; cf. *ho huios mou, ho eklelegmenos* of Luke 9:35); Paul uses *ho heautou huios* (Rom 8:3), *ho idios huios* (Rom 8:32), *morphe* (Phil 2:6), *eikon* (Col 1:15), and *prototokos* (Rom 8:29; Col 1:15,18) in speaking of Christ's relation to God. Only John uses *monogenes* as an adjective or substantive in depiction of that relationship.
2 For the relevant literature, see F. Kattenbusch, 'Only Begotten', in *Dictionary of Christ and the Gospels*, ed. J. Hastings (1908), 2:282–2.

3 F. Büchsel plays down this overlapping of ideas by saying: 'If the LXX has different terms for *yaḥid*, this is perhaps because different translators were at work' (*Theological Dictionary of the New Testament*, IV, ed. G. Kittel, trans. G. W. Bromiley [1967], p. 739). Admittedly, a number of translators were involved. Yet the fact that *yaḥid* can be translated by both *monogenes* and *agapetos* suggests something of the roughly synonymous connotations associated with these two Greek words.

4 Roman poets spoke of the Phoenix as a 'unica' or 'semper unica' bird; later Greek Christians (for example, Origen, Cyril, the Apostolic Constitutions 5.7) continued to refer to the Phoenix as *monogenes*.

5 Cf. also 1 Enoch 105:2, though this is probably a Christian interpolation, and 4 Ezra 7:28–29; 13:32; 37, 52; 14:9, though 4 Ezra dates from the first part of the second century AD.

6 Contra G. Dalman, *The Words of Jesus*, trans. D. M. Kay (Edinburgh: T. & T. Clark, 1909), pp. 271–2; W. Bousset, *Kyrios Christos* (Göttingen: Vandenhoerk & Ruprecht, 1913), pp. 53–4; and R. Bultmann, *Primitive Christianity in its Contemporary Setting*, trans. R. H. Fuller (London: Thames & Hudson, 1956), pp. 176–7.

7 W. Kümmel points out that a major interest of Matthew is 'the proof that Jesus is "the Christ, the Son of the living God" (16.16)' (*Introduction to the New Testament*, trans A. J. Mattill, Jr [Nashville: John Knox, 1965], p. 83).

8 'Son of God': Rom 1:4; 2 Cor 1:19; Gal 2:20; 'the Son' (or, 'his Son'): Rom 1:3,9; 5:10; 8:3,29,32; 1 Cor 1:9; 15:28; Gal 1:16; 4:4,6; 1 Thess 1:10. W. Kramer observes: 'In comparison with the passages in which the titles 'Christ Jesus' or 'Lord' occur, this is an infinitesimally small figure' (*Christ, Lord, Son of God*, trans. B. Hardy [London: SCM, 1966], p. 183). Kramer further notes that 'Paul's use of the title "Son of God" depends primarily on external factors, in that it is prompted by what has gone before' (ibid, p. 185).

9 Contra G. Dalman (*Words of Jesus*, pp. 274–5), *et al.* Likewise, the separation of the titles 'Christ' and 'Son of God' in Luke 22:67–71 and Acts 9:20–2 may be similarly understood.

10 Cf. also the quotation of Hos 11:1 in Matt 2:15.

11 Cf. E. Lövestam, *Son and Saviour: A Study of Acts 13:32–37*, trans. M. J. Petry (Lund: Gleerup, 1961), who argues in the body of his book that 'the covenant promise to David of permanent dominion for his house and its fulfilment in Jesus the Messiah has a dominating place in Paul's sermon in Acts 13:16ff.' (p. 84), and in an appendix on ' "Son of God" in the Synoptic Gospels' that 'the royal aspect plays a very important role in the designation of Jesus as "God's Son" in the Synoptics' (p. 110).

12 Cf. J. Jeremias, *The Central Message of the New Testament* (London: SCM, 1965), pp. 9–30; *idem, The Prayers of Jesus*, trans. J. Bowden

(London: SCM, 1967), pp. 11–65; *New Testament Theology*, I: *The Proclamation of Jesus*, trans. J. Bowden (London: SCM, 1971), pp. 61–8.

13 Baptism: Matt 3:17; Mark 1:11; Luke 3:22; Transfiguration: Matt 17:5; Mark 9:7.

14 Luke 9:35 (Transfiguration).

15 Or *theos* in John 1:18, which is externally better attested (P[66], P[75], ℵ, B, C, etc.) and corresponds internally to John's use of *huios* to signal primarily Jesus's divine nature.

12 WHEN 'LITERAL' IS NOT ACCURATE

Herbert M. Wolf

The goal of a good translation is to provide an accurate, readable rendition of the original which will capture as much of the meaning as possible. According to E. A. Speiser, 'the terms and thoughts of the original . . . the nuances of meaning, and the shadings of emphasis should all be transposed from one medium into another without leaving any outward sign of the transfer'.[1] This is a difficult task and cannot be accomplished with perfection, not even if the work being translated is the Bible itself. Languages simply do not correspond to one another so closely that nothing is lost in translation. Anyone who has gained facility in a foreign language knows that certain terms or idioms cannot be transferred into English without some modification. English – like any other language – cannot capture all the nuances and shades of meaning contained in another language.

When it comes to translations of the Bible, we can observe two extremes. One kind of translation emphasises a literal, word-for-word rendition that tries to preserve the grammatical and syntactical features of the Hebrew and Greek. Such a translation favours the source language over the receptor language and – while it may claim to be a very accurate translation – it sometimes misses important nuances of meaning and is hard to read easily. The other approach pays little attention to strict grammatical correspondence and attempts to convey the general idea found

176

in a particular sentence. By striving to produce a smooth and readable translation, such a version often favours the second medium at the expense of the source language and is really a paraphrase rather than a translation.[2]

In the Preface to the NIV, the Committee on Bible Translation states that sometimes it was necessary to modify sentence structure and to move away from a word-for-word translation in order to be faithful to the thought of the biblical writers and to produce a truly accurate translation. Since its publication, however, a number of observers have criticised the less literal approach of the NIV and have pointed to 'interpretational intrusions' foisted upon the text.[3] While it may be true that at times the NIV translators have been guilty of reading something into the text, I would contend that overall this version has achieved a high level of accuracy by its philosophy of translation. By occasionally moving away from a literal translation, they have produced a more accurate translation that captures the meaning of the original languages with greater precision. In the pages that follow, I shall present several examples that illustrate how a literal translation can at times be misleading rather than helpful.

CASES INVOLVING AN UNUSUAL OR TECHNICAL MEANING FOR A WORD

In a significant number of cases, a word or term that normally has a clearly defined range of meaning will be used in a context that calls for an unexpected translation. For example, the Hebrew word *nephesh* usually means 'soul', 'person' or 'life', but in Numbers 5:2 and 6:6 it refers to a 'dead body' and the ceremonial uncleanness associated with proximity to a corpse. Here the NIV agrees with other translations that employ 'dead body' or 'dead', as in the KJV. The NASB, however, prefers 'dead person' in its desire to be consistent in its handling of *nephesh*.

Another common word, *zera'*, usually means 'seed,

offspring, descendants'; yet in Isaiah 1:4 the NIV renders it 'brood' in the phrase 'a brood of evildoers'. This is a verse describing the rebellion of Israel and contains four phrases that depict the sinfulness of the nation. Many commentators feel that the term 'offspring of evildoers' is an appositional genitive that means 'offspring who are evildoers' and not 'the children of evildoers'.[4] Isaiah is not focusing upon the wickedness of the parents as much as the sin of the current generation. By using the slightly less literal 'brood of evildoers', the NIV helps the reader see this distinction which otherwise could easily be missed. Compare Jesus's description of the Pharisees as 'You snakes! You brood of vipers!' in Matthew 23:33.

Long before Isaiah, the Israelites were guilty of rebelling against the Lord when they worshipped the golden calf at Mount Sinai. In the midst of their idolatry they offered sacrifices and then 'sat down to eat and to drink, and rose up to play' (Exod 32:6, KJV). The NIV changes 'play' to 'indulge in revelry' because in all likelihood the celebration involved dancing and sexual immorality. Orgies of this sort often accompanied pagan worship in the ancient world. Paul quotes Exodus 32:6 in 1 Corinthians 10:7, and again the NIV expands 'play' to 'indulge in pagan revelry'.[5] The next verse goes on to describe the sexual immorality connected with the worship of the Baal of Peor in Numbers 25:1–9.

The book of Proverbs also contains several verses where non-literal translations enhance accuracy. In both Proverbs 8:18 and 21:21 the word *ṣᵉdaqah* – normally rendered 'righteousness' – is translated 'prosperity', perhaps understood as the reward of righteous living (cf. 15:6). In 8:18 *ṣᵉdaqah* is linked with riches and enduring wealth, and in 21:21 with finding life and honour. The abstract quality of 'righteousness' does not seem to fit either verse.[6]

An understanding of Hebrew parallelism also assists us in solving the translation problem found in Proverbs 2:16. In this verse, a young man is warned to stay away from the 'stranger' or 'foreigner' who will seduce him. At first, it looks as if the writer is warning Israelites against inter-marrying with foreign women, whose idolatry often lured them away from worshipping the Lord, the way the wives of Solomon did (cf. 1 Kings 11:1). But further study reveals that 'stranger' and 'foreigner' appear in parallel lines four more times in Proverbs (5:10,20; 7:5; 27:2), and none of these verses points to a non-Israelite setting. In fact, 27:2 seems to use the pair in a general way: 'Let another [literally "a stranger"] praise you, and not your own mouth;/some-one else [literally "a foreigner"], and not your own lips.' Moreover, in Proverbs 6:24 'foreigner' is parallel to 'im-moral woman', and in 23:27 it is linked to 'prostitute'. Since according to 7:19 this woman is married, it is evident that 'stranger' or 'foreigner' refers to any adulteress – whether Israelite or not – and that a relationship with her is to be considered off-limits.[7] To make this clear, the NIV uses 'adulteress' to translate 'stranger', and 'wayward wife' in place of 'foreigner'. Other translations also use 'adulteress' in these verses (cf. NASB and NAB); the RSV contains the words 'loose woman' and 'adventuress' in 2:16; 5:20 and 7:5, and the NKJV uses 'immoral woman' and 'seductress'. Although these renderings are not as literal as 'stranger' or 'foreigner', they convey the meaning of the text more precisely.

In the New Testament the apostle Paul similarly de-nounced sexual immorality as one of 'the works of the flesh' (Gal 5:19, KJV). The conflict between living by the Spirit or by the flesh is emphasised in Galatians 5 and in Romans 7–8. In order to show that 'flesh' refers not to the body but to the sinfulness of man, the NIV has often rendered 'flesh' (*sarx*) as 'sinful nature' (see Rom 8:3–5, 8–9). While many readers would properly understand 'flesh' in the sense of 'human weakness', the translation 'sinful nature' avoids any misinterpretation of this key theological term.

Another important theological term that poses problems for the translator is the *arrabon pneumatos*, the 'pledge' or 'guarantee' of the Spirit referred to in Ephesians 1:14 and 2 Corinthians 1:22 and 5:5. *Arrabon* is a loanword taken from the Hebrew *'erabon*, a 'pledge' or 'guarantee of payment' used of the seal and staff given by Judah to Tamar in return for her services (Gen 38:17,18,20).[8] This 'pledge' was a guarantee that he would make full payment the following day. According to Ephesians 1:13–14 the Holy Spirit is the seal 'who is a deposit guaranteeing our inheritance' (NIV). Other translations have 'who is the guarantee of our inheritance' (RSV, NKJV) or 'the pledge of our inheritance' (NASB, JB). In 2 Corinthians 1:22 and 5:5 the same term refers again to the Holy Spirit 'as a deposit, guaranteeing what is to come'. While 'pledge' would be the most literal rendering, the difficulty we have in grasping the cultural background of the term argues for an expanded translation.

CASES IN WHICH ADDING A WORD OR PHRASE HELPS CLARIFY THE MEANING

In a number of instances, the translation of a particular term is improved greatly by the addition of a word or phrase that, strictly speaking, is not found in the original language. For example, in response to Mary's observation that there was no more wine at the wedding in Cana, Jesus addressed her as 'Woman' (John 2:4). Without any further qualifications 'Woman' sounds abrupt and almost discourteous, but since Jesus used the same word as he spoke to his mother from the cross in John 19:26 (literally 'Woman, here is your son'), there is no doubt that this form of address expressed deep love and respect.[9] The NIV seeks to convey this warmth by translating both passages as 'Dear woman'. Compare the RSV, which uses 'O woman', and the NEB, which has 'mother' instead of 'woman'.

In an important chapter dealing with marriage, the apostle Paul stated that it is good for some people to remain single, but those who lack self-control ought to marry, 'for it is better to marry than to burn' (1 Cor 7:9, KJV). Most interpreters feel that 'burn' refers to the flames of passion that can only rightly be satisfied in marriage. To make this clear, both the NIV and the NKJV translate the verb 'to burn with passion'. The RSV uses 'to be aflame with passion' and the JB has 'to be tortured'.

Deep emotions are also involved in worship, and Job 31:27 provides an interesting example of how this functions in a pagan context. In this chapter Job has been vigorously defending his innocence of the charges made by his three 'comforters' and verses 26–7 assert that he has never been guilty of worshipping the sun or moon. Those whose hearts were enticed by the heavenly bodies on occasion 'offered them a kiss of homage' (NIV). Literally the text says 'my mouth has kissed my hand'. But since kissing a god was a common act of worship (cf. 1 Kings 19:18; Hos 13:2), there is little doubt that Job is talking about throwing a kiss of adoration and homage in the direction of the sun or moon.

In 1 Thessalonians 1:3 Paul praises the believers for their 'work of faith and labour of love and steadfastness of hope' (NASB). These three genitive phrases that use the common triad of faith, hope and love (see 1 Cor 13:13) are handled as subjective genitives by the NIV, and the relationship between the two nouns in each unit is made very explicit: 'your work produced by faith, your labour prompted by love, and your endurance inspired by hope.' Dana and Mantey say that in a subjective genitive 'the noun in the genitive *produces* the action', as in the sentence 'Christ's love compels us' (2 Cor 5:14).[10] Perhaps the phrase 'labour of love' would be understood without adding 'prompted by', but it is unlikely that 'work of faith' is as clear to the English reader as 'work produced by faith'.[11] Besides, 'work of faith' could be taken erroneously to mean that faith itself is a work.

For those readers whose endurance is strong enough to take them through Leviticus 13 and 14, the final sentence of chapter 14 must look like pure paraphrase when compared with other versions. How does one go from 'This is the law of leprosy' (KJV, NASB) to 'These are the regulations for infectious skin diseases and mildew' (NIV)? The problem lies mainly in the translation of the Hebrew word ṣara'at, which refers to a number of skin diseases not necessarily connected with Hansen's disease. To complicate the matter, clothing and houses can also be afflicted in an analogous manner, so the word can also mean 'mildew' or 'mould' (cf. Lev 13:47; 14:34). When the text comes to the final summary in Leviticus 14:57, ṣara'at, traditionally 'leprosy', refers to the regulations about houses and clothing as well as about skin diseases. The only way to make this clear is to add 'mildew' to the translation. Without it the translation might be more literal but less accurate, and Leviticus needs all the clarity we can muster. Compare the NEB which reads, 'This is the law for skin-disease, mould, and fungus.'

On occasion a word or phrase must be added to the translation because the antecedent to a pronoun is ambiguous. This is probably more of a problem with Hebrew than Greek, and one of the best examples comes from Psalm 44:2 (Hebrew 3). In the KJV the verse reads, 'How thou didst drive out the heathen with thy hand and plantedst them; how thou didst afflict the people, and cast them out.' The NIV has 'With your hand you drove out the nations/ and planted our fathers;/ you crushed the peoples/ and made our fathers flourish.' The NIV replaces 'them' with 'our fathers' in lines two and four, and changes 'cast out' to 'made flourish'. The key to the problem is the verb shillaḥ, which literally means 'to send out' or 'let loose' and is the word used in Exodus as Moses tells Pharaoh, 'Let my people go' (8:1 [Hebrew 7:26]; 9:1; 10:3). But it is also the word used in Psalm 80:11 (Hebrew 12), where God 'sent out' the boughs of the vine to the Mediterranean Sea. Psalm 80 affords an excellent parallel to Psalm 44 because it speaks of driving out the nations in verse 8 (cf. Ps 44:2) and of planting the nation of Israel as a vine. Thus both 'plant' and 'send out' appear in Psalm 44:2 and Psalm 80:8 and 11, demonstrating that the antecedent of 'them' in Psalm 44:2 is Israel or 'our fathers' taken from verse 1. God drove the nations out of Canaan, but he planted Israel as a vine that

extended to the west and the north. The NASB is technically correct with the translation 'Then thou didst plant
them' and 'Then thou didst spread them abroad', but it is
unclear whether these lines refer to the nations or to Israel
or whether 'spread abroad' is a positive extension or a
negative scattering. Since Psalm 80:8–11 shows convincingly that the spreading out is indeed positive, the NIV's
use of 'made flourish' is an apt translation.

CASES IN WHICH SENTENCE STRUCTURE
HAS BEEN CHANGED

Since no two languages express ideas in the same way,
sometimes it is necessary to change one or more grammatical forms in order to translate a sentence properly. Nouns
may be translated as verbs, or perhaps conjunctions as
prepositions. One of the simplest changes is to combine
two terms that really function as one unit. An example of
such a hendiadys is found in Deuteronomy 7:9, where God
is described as one who keeps 'the covenant and the love'
(or 'lovingkindness'). The word 'love' (*hesed*) is often used
in connection with covenant (for example, Ps 89:28
[Hebrew 29]) and indicates a firm commitment to the
covenant relationship. Hence, the NIV translates the two as
one expression, 'his covenant of love'. Compare the NAB,
which accomplishes the same thing by using an adjective:
'his merciful love'. Neither the RSV ('who keeps covenant
and steadfast love') nor the NASB ('who keeps His
covenant and His lovingkindness') chooses to combine the
terms.

Another example of the same phenomenon is found in
Isaiah 1:13, where God declares that he cannot stand
'iniquity and solemn assembly'. As Israel's wickedness
increased, even their sacred meetings were tainted with
sin.[12] To bring out the interrelatedness of the two terms,
the NIV makes the first noun an adjective: 'I cannot bear
your evil assemblies.' Consistent with its handling of

Deuteronomy 7:9, the RSV stays with 'I cannot endure iniquity and solemn assembly'.

There are two important New Testament passages dealing with faith whose meaning is likewise sharpened by changes in sentence structure. One is Galatians 3:2 and 5, two verses which both contain the phrases *ex ergon nomou*, 'by the works of the law', and *ex akoes pisteos*, 'by the hearing of faith'. In the first phrase the NIV changes the noun 'works' into the verbal noun 'observing', while in the second phrase it reverses both the position and the grammatical function of 'hearing' and 'faith'. 'Hearing' becomes 'what you heard' and 'faith' is changed to 'believing'. The sentence now reads: 'Did you receive the Spirit by observing the law, or by believing what you heard?' Each modification seems to make it easier for the reader to receive the full impact of the verse. Other translations achieve clarity by changing 'by the hearing of faith' (KJV) to 'by hearing with faith' (NASB, NKJV), 'by believing the gospel message' (NEB), or 'because you believed what was preached to you' (JB).

Perhaps the most famous verse on faith is Hebrews 11:1: 'Now faith is the substance of things hoped for, the evidence of things not seen' (KJV). Written almost in the form of Hebrew parallelism, this verse introduces a chapter that catalogues the heroes of the faith. By changing the noun 'substance' to 'assurance' – a meaning also found in 3:14 – and 'evidence' to 'conviction', the NASB improves considerably upon the KJV. The NIV follows the lead of the TEV by changing the two nouns to the adjectives 'sure' and 'certain': 'Now faith is being sure of what we hope for and certain of what we do not see.' Nothing has been added to the text, and yet these slight changes make the verse so much clearer.

CASES INVOLVING IDIOMATIC EXPRESSIONS

Although a number of examples from the preceding categories could also be treated as idioms, there are some verses that illustrate this phenomenon better than others. One of the most difficult idioms to translate is found in the opening line of Amos 4:6, where the Lord gives his people 'cleanness of teeth in all your cities' (KJV). Since the nation refused to repent, God sent a famine upon the land, and there was little or no food to get caught between the teeth. In our culture 'cleanness of teeth' connotes a bright smile, so some translations move away from a literal rendering. The NAB has 'Though I have made your teeth clean of food' and the NEB reads, 'It was I who kept teeth idle.' The NIV leaves out 'teeth' entirely and says, 'I gave you empty stomachs', though the literal 'cleanness of teeth' is kept as a footnote.

Another verse that deals with food is Proverbs 15:17: 'Better a meal of vegetables where there is love/ than a fattened calf with hatred.' 'Fattened calf' is literally 'an ox of the stall', because animals kept in the stall could be fed large amounts of fodder and fattened before slaughter. These animals were reserved for special occasions such as a wedding feast (cf. Matt 22:4) or a family celebration (cf. Luke 15:23). Amos condemns the wealthy men of Israel who lounge on their couches and 'dine on choice lambs and fattened calves' (6:4), while they ignored the prophet's call to repentance. Again, these are 'calves from the midst of the stall'. Almost all translations use either the word 'fattened' (NASB, JB, NIV), 'fatted' (RSV, NKJV) or 'fat' (NEB) in Proverbs 15:17. By such a rendering, they avoid the lack of clarity found in the KJV with its 'stalled ox'.

The verb 'to know' and the noun 'knowledge' have many uses in the Bible, one of which serves to describe sexual intercourse. When Genesis 4:1 says that 'Adam knew Eve his wife' (KJV), it clearly refers to marital relations. More often the verb is used of virgins, such as Lot's daughters 'which have not known man' (Gen 19:8, KJV) or the girls who were taken as plunder after all the males and non-virgins were killed in battle (cf. Num 31:17–18,35; Judg 21:12). In Numbers and Judges the verb is qualified by a phrase that makes the sexual aspect more explicit. They 'had not known a man by lying with him' (Judg 21:12, NASB). Genesis 19:5 also uses the verb with reference to the homosexual urges of the men of Sodom. They wanted Lot to bring the men out 'that we may know them' (KJV). There is little doubt that this means 'so that we can have sex with them' (NIV). Other translations use 'have intercourse' (NEB), 'have relations' (NASB), or 'know them *carnally*' (NKJV).

The book of Hosea does not employ the word 'know' in a sexual sense, but by way of analogy it refers to Israel's failure to know the Lord as her covenant husband. In chapters 1–3 Hosea describes the unfaithfulness of his wife Gomer, and her adultery pictures the way Israel deserted the Lord and chased after other gods. Yet God looked forward to the day when he would 'betroth [Israel] in faithfulness,/ and [Israel] will acknowledge the LORD' (Hos 2:20 [Hebrew 22], NIV). 'Acknowledge' could also be translated 'know' and plays on the intimate relationship of husband and wife.[13]

Because of the nature of language, an idiom cannot always be translated the same way in every context. Sometimes at least a slight modification is necessary to enhance communication. To illustrate this point, let us consider the Hebrew expression 'speak to the heart'. This is best known from Isaiah 40:2, where the prophet is told, 'Speak tenderly to [literally "Speak to the heart of"] Jerusalem' (NIV). This translation is also very appropriate for Shechem's words to Jacob's daughter Dinah, the girl he loved (Gen 34:3). But 'speak tenderly' is perhaps not masculine enough for Joseph's conversation with his brothers, so the NIV says that he 'spoke kindly to them' (Gen 50:21). When the idiom is used by a king trying to prepare his troops for a battle against overwhelming odds, the NIV says that Hezekiah 'encouraged them with these words' (2 Chron 32:6). Hezekiah also 'spoke encouragingly to all the Levites' when he assembled them to lead the nation in a Passover observance that had long been neglected (2 Chron 30:22).

Turning now to the New Testament, we will look finally

at two passages from the Gospel of John. The first example is John 1:13, a verse replete with interpretation problems as it describes children born of God, 'born, not of blood, nor of the will of the flesh, nor of the will of man, but of God' (KJV, NASB). These three negative expressions are very literal but equally difficult to grasp, so the NIV has changed them to 'not of natural descent, nor of human decision or a husband's will'. There is little doubt that 'blood' (or 'bloods') refers to natural birth and that either the second or third expression refers to sexual desire.[14] The NEB combines the two with 'or by the fleshly desire of a human father'. 'Flesh' is not an easy concept to work with, however, as we noted in category one, and Arndt and Gingrich connect *sarx* in this instance with the sexual urge, but with no implication of any sinful desire.[15] Thus the NIV uses the more neutral term 'human' rather than 'fleshly.'

Although Jesus's reference to his mother as 'Dear woman' has already been discussed in category two, let us return to John 2:4 and examine the question Jesus poses to Mary: 'Dear woman, why do you involve me?' Literally the words mean 'What is to you and to me?' – not a very helpful translation, to be sure. The idiom is derived from a Hebrew expression which occurs several times in the Old Testament. Twice it is used when David disagrees with a soldier's advice, and the NIV says (2 Sam 16:10; 19:22 [Hebrew 23]): 'What do you and I have in common, you sons of Zeruiah?' When the wicked king of Israel asked Elisha for the word of the Lord, the prophet responded, 'What do we have to do with each other?' as he reluctantly inquired of the Lord on the king's behalf (2 Kings 3:13). An even stronger adversarial relationship is indicated by the question of the two demon-possessed men when Jesus came to the region of the Gadarenes (Matt 8:29): 'What do you want with us, Son of God?' They wanted to be left alone until the judgment day.

From these other verses one can see the wide variety of contexts in which this idiom occurs, and the various versions translate these verses with considerable flexibility. In the case of John 2:4 the issue is complicated by the close relationship between Mary and Jesus. Is Jesus saying 'What do you want with me?' or 'What business is that of ours?' or 'What authority do you have over me?'[16] Again the major versions handle the idiom in a variety of ways. The NEB says, 'Your concern, mother, is not mine'; the NKJV reads, 'Woman, what does your concern have to do with Me?' and the JB has, 'Woman, why turn to me?' The precise shade of meaning is difficult to determine, but these idiomatic translations are a considerable improvement over a literal rendering.

Granted, no version that aims at accuracy is eager to depart from a literal translation too often. Believers want to know what the Bible says as well as what it means. But, as the examples in this chapter have tried to show, at times it is necessary to move away from a literal translation so that the message of the Scriptures can be clearly communicated. The NIV has been very cautious when it has departed from a 'literal' rendering, but its willingness to do so has markedly enhanced its overall accuracy.

NOTES

1 *Genesis*, Anchor Bible (Garden City, NY: Doubleday, 1964), p. lxiii.
2 Ibid., pp. lxiii–lxiv.
3 See E. L. Miller, 'The New International Version and the Prologue of John', *Harvard Theological Review* (July–October, 1979): 310.
4 E. J. Young, *The Book of Isaiah* (Grand Rapids: W. B. Eerdmans, 1965), 1:45–6.
5 Cf. W. Harold Mare, 'First Corinthians', in *The Expositor's Bible Commentary* (Grand Rapids: Zondervan, 1976), 10:249. The RSV uses 'dance' in 1 Cor 10:7.
6 See Herbert M. Wolf, 'Interpreting Wisdom Literature', in *The Literature and Meaning of Scripture*, ed. Morris A. Inch and C. Hassell Bullock (Grand Rapids: Baker Book House, 1981), p. 67.

7 Ibid., pp. 70–2.
8 See BDB, p. 786, and Ronald B. Allen in *Theological Wordbook of the Old Testament*, ed. R. L. Harris, G. L. Archer and B. K. Waltke (Chicago: Moody Press, 1980), pp. 693–4.
9 Also cf. John 20:15; cf. Merrill C. Tenney in *The Expositor's Bible Commentary*, 9:42.
10 H. F. Dana and Julius R. Mantey, *A Manual Grammar of the Greek New Testament* (New York: Macmillan, 1927), p. 78.
11 Cf. Robert L. Thomas in *The Expositor's Bible Commentary*, 11:241.
12 Young, *Isaiah*, 1:66.
13 Cf. *NIV Study Bible*, pp. 1321–2, 1325.
14 Cf. Henry Alford, *The Greek Testament*, rev. by Everett F. Harrison (Chicago: Moody Press, 1958), 1:684–5.
15 AG, p. 752.
16 Tenney, in EBC, 9:42.

13   ANGLICISING THE NIV

Donald J. Wiseman

The decision to publish a British and Commonwealth edition of *The Holy Bible: New International Version* (NIV) to coincide with the first American issue of the complete Bible in 1978 was farsighted, yet raised the whole question of 'Anglicisation'. This term denotes 'to make English in form and character', but in Bible translation it has come to mean the adoption of the English spelling, vocabulary and usages common to British, as distinct from American, readers.

The debate about the linguistic differences between the 'Queen's English' and that used across the Atlantic still continues; a recent leading article in the London *Times* stressing the increasing divergence adopted the view that within a hundred years each would be unintelligible to the other. This does not take into account the unifying force of the Scriptures, which have long been part of the common bond, initially based on the seventeenth-century *King James Version* (KJV), commonly called in Britain the *Authorised Version* (AV). Close alliance in the Second World War and the media, primarily films and radio, with such mediating broadcasters as Alistair Cooke and popular journals like the *Reader's Digest* bridging any linguistic barrier, have broadened the vocabulary of both parties.

The *Revised Standard Version New Testament* in 1946 circulated at first with American spellings, but with the increasing acceptance in the United Kingdom the whole Bible published in 1952 was given modified spellings and some

190

vocabulary changes. When the so-called common language *Today's English Version* (TEV) New Testament was issued by Collins in 1966, this followed the same practice. However, when the British (& Foreign) Bible Society in London published the complete Bible (*Good News Bible*: GNB) ten years later, it judged it essential that a more thorough Anglicisation be made. This was effected by some half a dozen individuals working under the overall coordination of Brynmar Price, who but rarely had to refer to that Society's 'Translations Advisory Group' for support and advice.

In England even before the advent of the RSV the need for a new translation into English from the Hebrew, Aramaic and Greek texts of the Bible had been voiced, among others by Dr William J. Martin of the University of Liverpool, as one of the aims of the Tyndale House for Biblical Research founded in Cambridge in 1945 (and not to be confused with the later Tyndale House publishing firm in the USA). But the dearth of competent scholars and other demands precluded this. Those evangelical scholars working on ancient Semitic and classical languages happily threw their lot in with the NIV project when this was first adumbrated. Among those was Martin himself, who was to make the work of the NIV the major task of his remaining years of life. His presence on the Committee on Bible Translation (CBT) of the NIV and the thorough work of literary consultants and the translators' realisation of 'the international use of English' that 'sought to avoid Americanisms on the one hand and obvious Anglicisms on the other' initially made the need for a special 'Anglicised Version' appear unnecessary and eventually prove to be limited in scope. Indeed it was not until after the trial work on *Proverbs and Ecclesiastes* (1977) that the matter really came to a head, though some changes in spelling in the NT NIV had been made for the UK edition.

In late 1977 it was decided that a British edition should appear simultaneously with the USA publication planned a year later. Professor Donald J. Wiseman of the University of

London, who had participated in the translation pro-
gramme from 1965, was asked to chair a group to effect the
necessary changes of text. He enlisted help, but little could
be done at first except set his assistants to work on the
unrevised latest stage of manuscript (CBT) in his hands. It
was not until May 1978 that the completed copy of the
text was available, since the CBT requested Rev. Youngve
Kindberg of New York International Bible Society (now
International Bible Society) not to send texts until they had
completed their final polishing and revision in February–
March. This meant that the Anglicising group had to work
fast under Wiseman's chairmanship.

The group included two specialists in English, Gordon
Humphreys, Headmaster of the renowned King Edward
School, Whitley and John Mighell-Smith. Paul Price, a
director of a large publishing firm and leading Baptist
layman, Grace B. Ruoff, a school teacher and ex-missionary
from Zambia, David Dowley and Winifred Marden of the
editorial staff of the Scripture Gift Mission, with extra
consultant help for designated books of the Old Testament,
completed the team.

A draft was finished by early June. Ed Palmer wisely
agreed with many of the changes himself to save time, the
bulk of proposals being sent to a special subcommittee of
the CBT whose approval was, however, not received in
London until early August, by which time the first printer's
proofs were being checked for consistency with CBT
revisions by the Rev. Ernest Lang and Beryl Barnes,
employed by Edward England of the publisher Hodder
& Stoughton, and by Wiseman. Additional points for
inclusion in the British edition were approved by CBT
even during this proofreading. In all these discussions a
number of translations suggested by the British team were
accepted for both editions. Despite printing and binding
delays, the publication date of 28 February 1979 was met
and celebrated by a service of thanksgiving and dedication
in the Church of St Martin-in-the Fields in Trafalgar Square,
with a large congregation drawn from many denomi-

nations. The decision to have this special edition has since been justified by the increasing acceptance and use of the NIV within the British Isles. Such 'Anglicisations' of Bibles originating in the USA have now become an established procedure in Britain.

The most numerous changes required for the British reader were the common variants in spelling as, for example, 'worshipped' for the American 'worshiped', 'labour' and 'neighbour' for 'labor' and 'neighbor', 'plough' for 'plow', and the like. While such alterations appear to be automatic, care was always needed to cover some variations in grammar and syntax; thus UK 'spat' for US 'spit' (past tense, Matt 26:27) and the addition of 'that' or 'so that' (593 times) after an active verb where this is omitted in American English. The American expression 'to have someone do something', for example, 'had him stand', was rendered into UK English 'made him stand'. Verbal forms vary, as American 'to rear' used of children against the common UK use of 'to rear' of animals and 'to bring up' of children.

The British preference for close definition by preposition accounts for 'due *to* his name' instead of 'due his name' (Ps 29:2) and 'given *to* him' instead of 'given him' (Ps 72:15). 'On behalf of' was substituted for the American 'in behalf of' (Mal 2:12, footnote). 'Ankles turn *over*' was used (2 Sam 22:37) since 'ankles turn' appears to state the obvious and not an accident or injury. Also the British say 'finish the week', not 'finish out the week' (Gen 29:27–28); so this has now been revised accordingly in both the British and the American editions.

Cultural differences required a number of changes, notably in legal expressions; for example, 'deeded' (Gen 23:17) was changed to 'legally made over'. 'Obligate' with the antiquated English sense of 'oblige' is rarely used and was changed to 'required to obey' (Gal 5:3) or 'bind' (Num 30:11). Similarly in legal contexts 'repealed' (Dan 6:8) is used almost only technically of the abolition or abrogation of a law passed by the Houses of Parliament; so 'annulled' was changed to 'repealed'. 'They put Jason and the others on bail and let them go' (Acts 17:9) stands for US 'they made Jason and the others post bond and let them go'. 'Ill-treat' was used for the less forcible 'mistreat' (Exod 22:21).

Expressions of duration and time vary, so that 'for forty years' was used for the American 'forty years' (Exod 16:35) in specifying the length of time of a given episode. In England the day could be divided into 'quarters' but not 'fourths', so Nehemiah 9:3 now reads 'quarter' instead of 'fourth'. Some words would not be understood in UK English, such as 'fieldstones' (hence 'stones from the field', Deut 27:6). The 'rooster' (Matt 26:34) is the British 'cock', the 'entry-way' the 'entrance' (Mark 14:68), the 'aide' the 'assistant' (Josh 1:1). 'Take care of your mat' (Acts 9:34) implies that the mat must not be forgotten or lost, whereas 'tidy up your mat' includes packing up for removal. 'Limber' was replaced by 'supple' (Gen 49:24), and 'firepot' (Gen 15:17) by 'brazier'.

Some biblical expressions have become so built into common quotations that to say 'I have escaped with only the skin of my teeth' (Job 19:20) would raise a smile, the British idiom being 'by only the skin of my teeth', which conjures up the danger of the situation and the 'close shave' experience of the escape. The 'ten thousand talents' and 'a hundred denarii' are explained in the footnotes to Matthew 18:24,28 as 'millions of pounds' (sterling) instead of 'millions of dollars' and 'a few pounds' instead of 'a few dollars', for the talent was worth several hundred pounds (Matt 25:15 footnote).

A difficult problem was posed by the differing usage of 'corn' and 'cornfields'. In the USA as in Canada and Australia, it means maize and Indian corn. In Britain, on the other hand, 'corn' means 'grain' and is normally wheat or barley (as in ancient Palestine). For this reason, 'heads of grain' was sometimes rendered 'ears of corn', the British term being retained for this aspect of the growth.

It was not always possible to Anglicise, so the sea cow or

dugong (Num 4:6), known in the far West but not in the colder Atlantic and European coastal waters, still reads quaintly in British ears, as does the katydid (Lev 11:22). None the less, all these changes are relatively minor, even if numerous, and in no way affect the literary style or significance and meaning of the text. That they have been allowed enables the widest range of readers of English to appreciate the Word of God for themselves without unnecessary linguistic barriers.

NOTE

The data to substantiate this paper are now lodged in the archives of the Bible Translation Department of the International Bible Society in East Brunswick, New Jersey, USA.

14 ISN'T THE KING JAMES VERSION GOOD ENOUGH? (THE KJV AND THE NIV COMPARED)

Edwin H. Palmer

I love the King James Version (KJV). I was converted under it. My first memory verses were taken from the KJV. I have been blessed by it. And God still uses the KJV. The way of salvation can still be found in the KJV.

But the KJV is not the best translation to use today. It served its purpose for its day. It was translated by godly men who did an excellent job with the tools they had and with the language of four centuries ago. Countless millions have been converted, sanctified and nurtured through it. Thank God for that marvellously-used translation.

But today the KJV will not do – and for two main reasons: (1) It adds to the Word of God, and (2) it has now-obscure and misleading renderings of God's Word.

THE KJV ADDS TO THE WORD OF GOD

The KJV translators did not intend to add to the Word of God. They did their best. But all they had to work with was a handful of copies of the Greek manuscripts of the New Testament books. And these were very late copies – about a thousand (!) years after the New Testament writers wrote. And in a few sections they had no Greek manuscript at all! Rather, they had to rely on the Latin Vulgate translation

196

of what they thought must have originally been in the Greek!

Because of the kindness and providence of God, many more Greek manuscripts had been preserved and were subsequently found – in fact, a little over 5,000 of them. And some were very old indeed, going back much further than the relatively few that the KJV translators used. Some went back to the four hundreds and three hundreds – even back to about AD 200. These were more reliable and accurate – not being corrupted by errors made during countless numbers of copyings, such as occurred with the late manuscripts used by the KJV.

As a result, we know today with a very high degree of accuracy what was in the original writings.[1] Uncertainty now exists in only an infinitesimally small part of the New Testament (the difference would be comparable to that between 'don't' and 'do not' or 'street' and 'way').

Here are some examples of verses that the KJV added to the Word of God, even though it did so unwittingly and in all innocence: Matt 17:21; 18:11; 23:14; Mark 7:16; 9:44,46; 11:26; 15:28; Luke 17:36; 23:17; John 5:4; Acts 8:37; 15:34; 24:7; 28:29; Rom 16:24; 1 John 5:7b–8a. These are just some of the whole verses that were added, and this list does not include the many phrases and words that were added.

A striking case of where the KJV, following bad Greek copies of the original, changed the original is John 1:18. The KJV says: 'No man hath seen God at any time; the only begotten Son, which is in the bosom of the Father, he hath declared him.' John 1:18, as inspired by the Holy Spirit, is one of those few clear and decisive texts that declare that Jesus is God. But, due to no fault of its own, the KJV, following inferior manuscripts, has altered what the Holy Spirit said through John. It calls Jesus 'Son', whereas it should have called him 'God'. To use the archaic language of the KJV, the verse should read this way: 'No man hath seen God at any time; the only begotten God, which is in the bosom of the Father, he hath declared him.' Or to say it in a modern and elegant way, 'No one has ever seen God, but God the One and Only [Son], who is at the Father's side, has made him known' (NIV).

Sometimes Evangelicals get excited because some of the modern paraphrases do not really give us the Word of God. They distort, alter and revise it. They are right to be concerned about this because they believe that the Bible is the very Word of God and they do not want any paraphrases to change what the Holy Spirit inspired. But they calmly go on reading the KJV, which in many places has added to (and so changed) God's very words. Such a practice is unfortunate.

THE KJV HAS NOW-OBSCURE AND MISLEADING RENDERINGS OF GOD'S WORD

This is so in part because some English words have changed their meaning since 1611. It is bad enough when translators have available only inferior copies of the original text of God's Word, but when, in addition to that, their translation of the Hebrew and Greek conveys erroneous ideas, the problem is compounded.

This is not to say that the KJV did not do an admirable job – for its time. We should thank God for it. Many of the examples of erroneous translations that are given below were not errors in 1611 when the KJV was published, but they are definitely errors today in view of the current meanings of those words. Other KJV errors are due to the translators' lack of knowledge in the seventeenth century.

Here are some examples of the now-misleading or obscure readings in the KJV:

1. Genesis 2:4. KJV: 'These are the generations of the heavens and of the earth.' The Hebrew term for 'generations' is an important one in Genesis and occurs ten times to mark new sections (2:4; 5:1; 6:9; 10:1; 11:10,27; 25:12,19; 36:1; 37:2). (It is repeated in Gen 36:9 for emphasis.) A preferable translation would be: 'This is the account of the heavens and the earth' (NIV).

2. Genesis 4:1. KJV: 'I have gotten a man from the LORD.' NIV: 'With the help of the LORD I have brought forth a man.'

3. Genesis 20:6. KJV: 'therefore suffered I thee not to touch her.' NIV: 'that is why I did not let you touch her.'

4. Genesis 21:31. KJV: 'Wherefore he called that place Beersheba; because there they sware both of them.' What did they 'sware'? 'Both of them'? No. Rather: 'So that place was called Beersheba, because the two men swore an oath there' (NIV).

5. Genesis 26:8. KJV: 'saw, and behold, Isaac was sporting with his wife.' NIV: 'saw Isaac caressing his wife.'

6. Genesis 26:10. KJV: 'one of the people might lightly have lien with thy wife.' NIV: 'One of the men might well have slept with your wife.'

7. Genesis 26:31. KJV: 'And they rose up betimes in the morning.' NIV: 'Early the next morning.'

8. Genesis 29:29–30. To whom does the 'he' refer in verse 30 of the KJV: '29 And Laban gave to Rachel his daughter Bilhah his handmaid, to be her maid. 30 And he went in also unto Rachel, and he loved also Rachel more than Leah, and served with him yet seven other years.' Who is the antecedent of 'he'? Laban, of course. But that is wrong. The Hebrew meant Jacob, so the NIV substituted 'Jacob' for 'he'. There are other confusions in this simple historical text. Who is the daughter – Bilhah or Rachel? Read the KJV again. Now the NIV: '29 Laban gave his servant girl Bilhah to his daughter Rachel as her maidservant. 30 Jacob lay with Rachel also, and he loved Rachel more than Leah. And he worked for Laban another seven years.' The NIV makes confusing pronouns clear by substituting the proper noun when necessary.

9. Genesis 30:27–9 is another case of confusion in the KJV: '27 And Laban said unto him . . . 28 And he said . . . 29 And he said unto him . . .' Who are those 'he's'? The most natural explanation would be Laban. But no. NIV: '27 But Laban said to him . . . 28 He added . . . 29 Jacob

said to him . . .' By using the word 'added' and substituting 'Jacob' for 'he' in verse 29, the KJV confusion is cleared up immediately.

10. Leviticus 13:47 (and other places in Lev 13 and 14). KJV: 'The garment also that the plague of leprosy is in.' A piece of cloth cannot have leprosy. So the KJV – and even some modern translations (Revised Standard Version, 'leprous disease'; New American Standard Bible, 'a mark of leprosy') – is misleading. It is better to translate: 'If any clothing is contaminated with mildew' (NIV).

11. Joshua 12:4. 'The coast of Og' (KJV) has nothing to do with water. It is 'the territory of Og' (NIV).

12. 2 Chronicles 2:2. KJV: 'told'. NIV: 'conscripted'.

13. 2 Chronicles 2:7. KJV: 'brass'. Brass was not known in Solomon's days; hence the NIV's 'bronze'.

14. 2 Chronicles 2:7. KJV: 'cunning to work in gold'. NIV: 'skilled to work in gold'.

15. 2 Chronicles 2:7. KJV: 'a man . . . that can skill to grave with the cunning men that are with me in Judah and in Jerusalem.' NIV: 'a man . . . experienced in the art of engraving, to work in Judah and Jerusalem with my skilled craftsmen.'

16. Nehemiah 1:5. KJV: 'the great and terrible God.' In 1611 the word 'terrible' meant 'awesome'. Today it usually means 'bad, wretched, full of terror', and therefore in contemporary English 'terrible' can be misleading. It should read: 'the great and awesome God' (NIV).

17. Job 20:3. KJV: 'I have heard the check of my reproach.' NIV: 'I hear a rebuke that dishonours me.'

18. Job 22:10–11. KJV: 'Therefore snares are round about thee, and sudden fear troubleth thee; or darkness, that thou canst not see; and abundance of waters cover thee.' The last half of this sentence has no clear meaning. Words just hang there between semicolons and a period. It is gobbledygook. NIV:

> That is why snares are all around you,
>   why sudden peril terrifies you,

why it is so dark you cannot see,
         and why a flood of water covers you.

Not only is the language of the NIV clear, but also the
format and poetry are beautiful.

19. Job 36:33. KJV: 'The noise thereof sheweth concerning it, the cattle also concerning the vapour.' NIV: 'His
thunder announces the coming storm; even the cattle make
known its approach.'

20. Psalm 67:3,5. KJV: 'people' (four times). The Hebrew
is not talking about separate individuals, but groups of
people, nations. Hence the NIV's 'peoples'. The difference
is only an 's', but what a difference in meaning!

21. Psalm 119:147. KJV: 'I prevented the dawning of the
morning.' NIV: 'I rise before dawn.'

22. Psalm 139:13. KJV: 'thou hast possessed my reins.'
NIV: 'For you created my inmost being.'

23. Isaiah 10:28. KJV: 'carriages'. NIV: 'supplies'.

24. Jeremiah 48:12. KJV: 'I will send unto him wander-
ers, that shall cause him to wander.' NIV: 'I will send men
who pour from jars, and they will pour her out.'

25. Ezekiel 21:24. KJV: 'discovered'. NIV: 'revealing'.

26. Ezekiel 24:17. KJV: 'tire'. NIV: 'turban'.

27. Amos 5:7. KJV: 'Ye who turn judgment to worm-
wood and leave off righteousness in the earth.' Dr Frank
Gaebelein thinks that one reason Evangelicals have been
slow in getting involved in a truly biblical social action is
that they have never understood the KJV in the many
places were it has used 'judgment' instead of 'justice'. What
is meant here in Amos 5:7 is not the juridical process of
making a decision, but justice, as the NIV makes clear: 'You
who turn justice into bitterness and cast righteousness to
the ground.' This misleading KJV translation is found in
many other places, such as Hos 2:19; 12:6; Amos 5:15; 6:12;
Mic 3:1,8,9; Hab 1:4; Zeph 3:5; Zech 7:9; Mal 2:17.

Think of how the KJV has held back the true meaning of
God's will when in the key verse of Amos (5:24) it says, 'But
let judgment run down as waters.' It should have said, 'But

let justice roll on like a river' (NIV). What a difference between judgment and justice!

28. Nahum 1:1. KJV: 'The burden of Nineveh.' NIV: 'An oracle concerning Nineveh.'

29. Matthew 11:25. KJV: 'At that time Jesus answered and said.' Jesus was not answering anybody here or in many other similar instances. Hence the NIV: 'Jesus said.' The KJV rendering creates an erroneous impression.

30. Matthew 17:25. KJV: 'Jesus prevented him' – an Old English way of saying 'Jesus was the first to speak' (NIV).

31. Matthew 20:31. KJV: 'And the multitude rebuked them, because they should hold their peace.' The 'because' makes no sense. NIV: 'The crowd rebuked them and told them to be quiet.'

32. Matthew 23:24. KJV: 'strain at a gnat'. What is meant is this: 'You strain out a gnat but swallow a camel' (NIV).

33. Matthew 26:27. KJV: 'Drink ye all of it.' This could be taken to mean that not a drop should be left. But that would be incorrect. NIV: 'Drink from it, all of you.'

34. Mark 2:3. KJV: 'sick of the palsy'. NIV: 'paralytic'.

35. Mark 4:38. KJV: 'Master'. Forty-six times the KJV uses the term 'master' when for today's reader it should use the term 'teacher'.

36. Mark 6:20. In the KJV Herod 'observed' John. It should be 'protected' (NIV).

37. Mark 6:25. KJV: 'by and by'. The Greek really means the opposite: 'right now' (NIV).

38. Luke 1:36. Luke does not say that Elizabeth was a 'cousin' of Mary as the KJV says, but a 'relative'.

39. Luke 1:40. Mary did not 'salute' (KJV) Elizabeth but 'greeted' her.

40. Luke 1:63. Zechariah did not ask for a 'writing table' (KJV) but for a 'writing tablet' (NIV).

41. Luke 23:15. In the KJV Pilate says of Jesus: 'and, lo, nothing worthy of death is done unto him'. What the Greek says is the exact opposite. Thus the NIV: 'as you can see, he has done nothing to deserve death.'

42. Acts 21:15. KJV: 'we took up our carriages'. NIV: 'we got ready'.

43. Acts 27:21. KJV: 'Sirs, ye should have hearkened unto me, and not have loosed from Crete, and to have gained this harm and loss.' NIV: 'Men, you should have taken my advice not to sail from Crete; then you would have spared yourselves this damage and loss.'

44. Acts 28:13. KJV: 'And from thence we fetched a compass.' A clearer translation: 'From there we set sail' (NIV).

45. Romans 1:17. KJV: 'For therein is the righteousness of God revealed.' How many Christians have failed to understand the great comfort of this verse because of the KJV's reading? Paul is not talking about God's righteousness, that is, his holy, righteous character, but a 'righteousness' that is provided by him through the life and death of Jesus Christ. This crucial passage should be translated: 'For in the gospel a righteousness from God is revealed' (NIV).

46. Romans 1:28. KJV: 'God gave them over to a reprobate mind, to do those things which are not convenient.' There are two problems here: First, Paul is not speaking of the reprobate, but of the 'depraved'. Second, Paul is not speaking of convenience at all. Instead, the verse would well be translated: 'he gave them over to a depraved mind, to do what ought not to be done.'

47. Romans 3:22. KJV: 'Even the righteousness of God which is by faith of Jesus Christ.' This is misleading on two counts: first, it is the righteousness that is from God, not his righteousness; second, it is faith in Christ, not 'faith of Christ'. It should read: 'This righteousness from God comes through faith in Jesus Christ' (NIV).

48. Romans 5:5. KJV: 'the Holy Ghost which is given unto us.' In 1611 'which' could be used of a person, but it is not normally so used today. In current English we say, 'the Holy Spirit, whom he has given us'.

49. Romans 14:23. KJV: 'And he that doubteth is damned.' That would ordinarily be understood to mean that the doubter goes to hell for ever. Not so the

Greek. It should be: 'But the man who has doubts is condemned.'

50. 1 Corinthians 4:4. KJV: 'For I know nothing by myself.' NIV: 'My conscience is clear.'

51. 1 Corinthians 5:3–5. One problem of the KJV is that its sentences ramble on and on, and are too complicated to figure out. The important passage, 1 Corinthians 5:3–5, is a case in point: '3 For I verily, as absent in body, but present in spirit, have judged already, as though I were present, concerning him that hath so done this deed, 4 in the name of our Lord Jesus Christ, when ye are gathered together, and my spirit, with the power of our Lord Jesus Christ, 5 to deliver such an one unto Satan for the destruction of the flesh, that the spirit may be saved in the day of the Lord Jesus.' What does 'in the name of our Lord Jesus Christ' go with? And who delivers such a one unto Satan? Paul? Corinthians? Who? It is not enough to get the general thrust of these verses. We should know precisely what God has said. One way is to shorten the sentences as the NIV does: '3 Even though I am not physically present, I am with you in spirit. And I have already passed judgment on the one who did this, just as if I were present. 4 When you are assembled in the name of our Lord Jesus and I am with you in spirit, and the power of our Lord Jesus is present, 5 hand this man over to Satan, so that the sinful nature may be destroyed and his spirit saved on the day of the Lord.'

52. 1 Corinthians 10:24. KJV: 'Let no man seek his own, but every man another's wealth.' The KJV could be understood as recommending coveting and perhaps stealing! A better translation would be: 'Nobody should seek his own good, but the good of others' (NIV).

53. 1 Corinthians 13. The KJV 'charity' does not mean philanthropy or almsgiving, but 'love'.

54. 1 Corinthians 16:22. 'If any man love not the Lord Jesus Christ, let him be Anathema Maranatha.' Who or what is 'Anathema Maranatha'? Someone forgot to put a full stop after 'Anathema', and to this day KJV Bibles have this error. Listen to the accuracy and clarity of the NIV: 'If

anyone does not love the Lord – a curse be on him. Come, O Lord!' After 'Lord' there is a note: 'In Aramaic the expression *Come, O Lord* is *Marana tha.*'

55. 2 Corinthians 2:17. KJV: 'For we are not as many, which corrupt the word of God.' NIV: 'Unlike so many, we do not peddle the word of God for profit.'

56. 2 Corinthians 4:2. KJV: 'dishonesty'. NIV: 'shameful ways.'

57. 2 Corinthians 5:21. KJV: 'For he hath made him to be sin for us, who knew no sin.' It was Jesus who knew no sin, not 'us'. It should be: 'God made him who had no sin to be sin for us' (NIV).

58. Ephesians 1:3. KJV: 'Blessed be the God and Father.' The word 'bless' is used in the KJV to mean (1) praise, (2) thanks, (3) to invoke God's favour, (4) happy. This is very confusing in today's English. In Ephesians, for example, what is meant by 'Blessed be the God and Father'? In 1 Corinthians 10:16, what is meant by 'blessing' when the KJV says, 'The cup of blessing which we bless, is it not the communion of the blood of Christ?'

The NIV attempted to be very careful so that there would not be confusion in this term that is traditionally and indiscriminately translated 'bless'. For the NIV, 'bless' means that someone in a higher position, such as God or a king, favours someone lower (cf. Heb 7:6–7). Hence in Psalm 67:7 the NIV reads, 'God will bless us' and in Genesis 28:6 Isaac 'blessed' his son Jacob. But in Ephesians 1:3 Paul 'praises' (NIV) God the Father. (When we want to praise a president for his actions, we don't say, 'I bless the president'.) And in 1 Corinthians 10:16 Paul says (in the NIV), 'Is not the cup of thanksgiving [not *blessing*] for which we give thanks [not *bless*] a participation in the blood of Christ?' The indiscriminate use of 'bless' and 'blessed' in the KJV is very confusing in today's English.

59. Ephesians 4:4. KJV: 'There is one body, and one Spirit, even as ye are called in one hope of your calling.' Here is an important verse and yet the statement 'ye are called in one hope of your calling' is confusing. Here is what

it means: 'just as you were called to one hope when you were called' (NIV).

60. Philippians 3:20. KJV: 'conversation'. NIV: 'citizenship'.

61. Philippians 4:14. KJV: 'Notwithstanding ye have well done, that ye did communicate with my affliction.' NIV: 'Yet it was good of you to share in my troubles.' It is obvious that the last part of the KJV sentence does not communicate ('ye did communicate with my affliction'), but it is also instructive to look at the first part to see how an unnatural word order causes the reader to stumble. It is not natural to say, 'ye have well done'. Nobody would talk like that today. Not only is the 'ye' unnatural, but also the 'have well done'. This sort of unnaturalness can be multiplied many times over, and it causes untold difficulties in the understanding and memorisation of God's Word.

62. 1 Thessalonians 1:4: KJV: 'your election of God'. In the days of the KJV, this was a way to say 'your election by God'. As it is today, the KJV suggests the opposite of what the Greek really says.

63. 1 Thessalonians 1:6. KJV: 'joy of the Holy Spirit'. Paul is not talking about the joy of the Holy Spirit, but the joy of the Thessalonians. What the KJV tried to convey was 'the joy given by the Holy Spirit' (NIV). One of the great causes of obscurity is the KJV's love for the preposition 'of', as was also seen in Romans 1:17 ('the righteousness of God'), Romans 3:22 ('faith of Jesus Christ') and 1 Thessalonians 1:4 ('your election of God'). In Greek it represents the genitive case, which has various usages that should be made specific in translation.

64. 1 Thessalonians 2:3. KJV: 'uncleanness'. NIV: 'impure motives'.

65. 1 Thessalonians 4:15. KJV: 'prevent'. NIV: 'precede'.

66. 1 Thessalonians 5:14. KJV: 'feebleminded'. The Greek, however, has nothing to do with being mentally deficient. Rather, it means being 'timid' (NIV).

67. 1 Thessalonians 5:22. KJV: 'Abstain from all appear-

ance of evil.' This involves a misunderstanding of the Greek idiom. Rather, 'Avoid every kind of evil' (NIV).

68. 2 Thessalonians 2:7. KJV: 'he who now letteth.' Today 'let' means 'allow, permit', but in 1611 one of its meanings was 'to hinder, obstruct, prevent' (still preserved in the legal phrase 'without let or hindrance' – and we still use 'let' in the KJV sense of holding back when in tennis we speak of a 'let' ball, that is, a ball that hits the net is invalid and must be served again). The NIV conveys the sense with 'the one who now holds it back.'

69. 1 Timothy 5:4. The KJV's 'nephews' is wrong. As we now know, the Greek word refers to 'grandchildren'.

70. 1 Timothy 6:5. KJV: 'supposing that gain is godliness'. This is entirely misleading. It should be: 'who think that godliness is a means to financial gain' (NIV).

71. 2 Timothy 1:15. KJV: 'This thou knowest, that all they which are in Asia be turned away from me.' Apart from the now-faulty grammar ('all they . . . be turned away'), it should be noted that 'Asia' does not mean Japan, China, Russia, India, Pakistan and Bangladesh. In Paul's day what was meant was a small 'province of Asia' (NIV). The unmodified word 'Asia' is misleading.

72. 2 Timothy 3:6. KJV: 'silly women'. NIV: 'weak-willed women'.

73. 2 Timothy 3:13. KJV: 'seducers'. NIV: 'impostors'.

74. Titus 1:6. The KJV's 'having faithful children' is wrong. 'Faithful' means having children who are loyal, reliable and worthy of trust. But what the Greek means is: 'a man whose children believe' (NIV).

75. Titus 2:13. The KJV wrongly distinguishes between God and Jesus ('the great God and our Saviour Jesus Christ'), whereas it should have called Jesus 'God' ('our great God and Saviour, Jesus Christ', NIV).

76. Hebrews 7:18. KJV: 'For there is verily a disannulling of the commandment going before for the weakness and unprofitableness thereof.' How can the Christian understand what the Holy Spirit said here? And who would want to memorise that? But listen to this accurate and clear

rendering: 'The former regulation is set aside because it was weak and useless' (NIV).

77. Hebrews 8:2. KJV: 'a minister of the sanctuary, and of the true tabernacle, which the Lord pitched.' The KJV misleads the reader to think that there is a sanctuary plus a true tabernacle. But this is wrong. Tabernacle is in apposition to sanctuary. Thus it should read: 'who serves in the sanctuary, the true tabernacle set up by the Lord' (NIV).

78. Hebrews 8:5. KJV: 'who serve unto the example and shadow of heavenly things.' What does that mean? More understandable is this: 'They serve at a sanctuary that is a copy and shadow of what is in heaven' (NIV).

79. Hebrews 8:12. KJV: 'For I will be merciful to their unrighteousness.' This seems to say that God is going to be good to unrighteousness. But the meaning is: 'For I will forgive their wickedness' (NIV).

80. Hebrews 8:13. KJV: 'In that he saith, A new covenant, he hath made the first old. Now that which decayeth and waxeth old is ready to vanish away.' What is the writer saying? Where does the quotation end – after 'covenant' or 'old' or 'away'? And what does 'waxeth' mean? Why should anyone who loves God's Word be kept in suspense? Why should he have to struggle to learn? Shouldn't the Bible be just as clear today as it was when it was given? What Hebrews 8:13 means is this: 'By calling this covenant "new", he has made the first one obsolete; and what is obsolete and ageing will soon disappear' (NIV).

81. Hebrews 9:1. KJV: 'Then verily the first covenant had also ordinances of divine service, and a worldly sanctuary.' Does 'divine service' mean 'God's work'? No. And what is a 'worldly sanctuary'? NIV: 'Now the first covenant had regulations for worship and also an earthly sanctuary.'

82. Hebrews 9:2–6. There is complete confusion in the KJV about what is the tabernacle, 'the first', 'the sanctuary' and the 'Holiest'.

83. Hebrews 9:10. KJV: 'which stood only in meats and drinks, and divers washings, and carnal ordinances, imposed on them until the time of reformation.' NIV: 'They

are only a matter of food and drink and various ceremonial washings – external regulations applying until the time of the new order.' Hebrews is a very important book with great truths about the relationship of the Old Testament sacrifices to Christ and the New Testament. It is imperative that Christians know what the Holy Spirit is saying to them.

84. James 5:11. KJV: 'patience of Job'. But Job was not patient. He was impatient; yet he persevered. Hence a better translation is 'Job's perseverance' (NIV).

85. 1 Peter 2:9. KJV: 'a peculiar people'. Today that means odd people. It should be 'a people belonging to God' (NIV).

86. 1 Peter 2:12. The KJV translates the Greek as 'Having your conversation honest' (using 'conversation' in the now-rare Latin sense of 'behaviour'). But the Greek says nothing at all about conversation or honesty ('honest' meant 'virtuous' or 'good' in 1611, but the meaning is now archaic). What it does say is: 'Live such good lives' (NIV).

87. 1 Peter 4:3. The KJV condemns 'banquetings' as being very evil. Today, of course, 'banqueting' is not sinful. Actually, what the KJV condemns is 'carousings' (NIV), for that is what 'banqueting' meant in 1611.

88. 2 Peter 1:1. KJV: 'the righteousness of God and our Saviour Jesus Christ.' NIV: 'the righteousness of our God and Saviour Jesus Christ.' The KJV translators certainly believed that Jesus was God, but, as we have already seen, in several important cases they obscured the New Testament witness to that truth.

89. 2 Peter 3:4. KJV: 'Where is the promise of his coming?' How odd that even some modern versions persist in this error (Revised Standard Version, New American Standard Bible, New English Bible)! The scoffers knew where the promise was – in the Bible and in the preaching of the apostles. They were not asking where the promise was. It was exactly because they knew where the promise was that they really asked, 'Where is the "coming" that he promised?' (NIV).

90. Jude 7. KJV: 'giving themselves over to fornication,

and going after strange flesh.' There are two problems here:
1. Since 'fornication' is ambiguous, the KJV is misleading.
2. What is 'strange flesh'? NIV: 'gave themselves up to sexual immorality and perversion.' The reader of the NIV realises that Jude is condemning all illegitimate sex.

91. Jude 19. KJV: 'These are they who separate themselves, sensual, having not the Spirit.' NIV: 'These are the men who divide you, who follow mere natural instincts and do not have the Spirit.'

This list of obscure or almost unintelligible KJV renderings could go on and on. Just to drive the point home even more clearly, what is the meaning of: chambering (Rom 13:13), champaign (Deut 11:30), chapiter (Jer 52:22), chapmen (2 Chron 9:14), chapt (Jer 14:4), charger (Matt 14:8 – it is not a horse), churl (Isa 32:7), cieled (Hag 1:4), circumspect (Exod 23:13), clouted upon their feet (Josh 9:5), cockatrice (Isa 11:8), collops (Job 15:27), confection (Exod 30:35 – it has nothing to do with sugar), cotes (2 Chron 32:28), covert (2 Kings 16:18), hoised (Acts 27:40), wimples (Isa 3:22), stomacher (Isa 3:24), wot (Rom 11:2), wist (Acts 12:9), withs (Judg 16:7), wont (Dan 3:19), suretiship (Prov 11:15), sackbut (Dan 3:5), the scall (Lev 13:30), scrabbled (1 Sam 21:13), roller (Ezek 30:21 – i.e., a splint), muffler (Isa 3:19), froward (1 Pet 2:18), brigadine (Jer 46:4), amerce (Deut 22:19), blains (Exod 9:9), crookbackt (Lev 21:20), descry (Judg 1:23), fanners (Jer 51:2), felloes (1 Kings 7:33), glede (Deut 14:13), glistering (Luke 9:29), habergeon (Job 41:26), implead (Acts 19:38), neesing (Job 41:18), nitre (Prov 25:20), tabret (Gen 31:27), wen (Lev 22:22)?

Having given many examples of obsolete English, let us look at two verses – verses that are typical and that do not have to do with doctrine – and see the unnaturalness of the English style, so that the reader's comprehension is hindered. One verse is Luke 14:10: 'But when thou art bidden, go and sit down in the lowest room; that when he that bade thee cometh, he may say unto thee, Friend, go up higher: then shalt thou have worship in the presence of them that sit at meat with thee' (KJV).

Here is a simple story that should be clear. But look at all the problems interfering with an easy comprehension of it.

a. There are five archaic, strange (to many Americans) terms and forms, such as 'thou', 'art', 'thee', 'cometh' and 'shalt'.

b. 'Bidden'. Today we say 'invited', not 'bidden'.

c. 'Room'. This is wrong. There were not different rooms. It means 'place'.

d. Today the semicolon is not used in this way.

e. 'Say unto.' Modern English: 'say to'.

f. The lack of quotation marks hinders the reader from knowing at a glance where the quotation stops.

g. 'Shalt thou.' Why a reverse order? In English, even with the archaic 'shalt' and 'thou', we would say, 'thou shalt'.

h. 'Have worship.' This is not the meaning at all. It means, rather, 'you will be honoured'.

i. The use of the colon here is wrong in today's English.

j. 'Them that sit at meat with thee.' A clearer reading: 'your fellow guests.'

Now read the NIV for clarity as well as beauty and dignity: 'But when you are invited, take the lowest place, so that when your host comes, he will say to you, "Friend, move up to a better place." Then you will be honoured in the presence of all your fellow guests.'

Luke penned a simple narrative, yet in the KJV translation are ten items that hinder a natural English style, and the modern meanings of three of the words are not what Luke intended.

This ought not to be. It is not being faithful to the original for today's English. Faithfulness demands that the Bible be just as clear, simple and natural as when the Holy Spirit inspired the original Hebrew and Greek. The KJV is now far from that.

Look at one more verse to see the unnaturalness and obscurity of style:

1 Corinthians 4:17: 'For this cause have I sent unto you Timotheus, who is my beloved son, and faithful in the

211

Lord, who shall bring you into remembrance of my ways which be in Christ, as I teach every where in every church.'

A much more difficult verse could have been selected, but this one is typical of the general style of the KJV: a part is almost unintelligible, and the rest is awkward.

Note what is almost unintelligible: 'as I teach every where in every church.' What does that 'as' mean? What is it comparing? Also, 'bring' is not clear to some readers. Note now the awkward language:

a. 'For this cause.' We do not talk like that today. It should be: 'For this reason.'

b. 'Have I sent.' We do not speak this way either. We say 'I have sent'.

c. 'Unto you.' We say 'to you'.

d. 'Timotheus.' Who is that? Well, why confuse? Why not say, 'Timothy'?

e. 'My beloved son.' Outside the KJV – except in marriage ceremonies, in churches that use KJV English, and in novels for the purpose of a literary effect – no one uses 'beloved'. Rather, we would say, 'my son whom I love'.

f. 'And faithful in the Lord.' The reader stumbles over this. To say 'who is faithful in the Lord' makes it much easier to read.

g. 'Who shall bring you into remembrance.' It is ill-advised and unfaithful to the spirit of the original to have such stilted and obsolete English for today's readers. How much simpler and more natural to say, 'who will remind you'.

h. 'My ways which be.' Even an English professor, let alone a first-grader, would not talk like this. Both would say, 'my ways which are'.

Read the KJV again and then this rendering: 'For this reason I am sending to you Timothy, my son whom I love, who is faithful in the Lord. He will remind you of my way of life in Christ Jesus, which agrees with what I teach everywhere in every church' (NIV).

These obscurities in 1 Corinthians 4:17 may seem insignificant. They do not deal with the heart of the gospel, and a

212

person can catch the general drift of what Paul is saying. But is that all we want? To catch the general drift of what God is saying to us? To know only the heart of the gospel?

If we believe that the Bible is God's Word – inspired and inerrant, an infallible guide for our lives – are we going to be satisfied with knowing generally and vaguely what God is saying, and only the central truths? Did not God give us his whole Word? Are the details of what God said unimportant? Is it not important to know everything that God said and with clarity?

Yet the KJV adds to (and so alters) God's Word, and it has now-obscure and misleading renderings of many verses. Scores of examples were given, but hundreds of others could have been given. For one who loves God and wants to know exactly what God says to him, a modern translation that is accurate and clear is necessary. Elsewhere I have written:

> Do not give them a loaf of bread, covered with an inedible, impenetrable crust, fossilised by three and a half centuries. Give them the Word of God as fresh and warm and clear as the Holy Spirit gave it to the authors of the Bible [. . .]
>
> For any preacher or theologian who loves God's Word to allow that Word to go on being misunderstood because of the veneration of an archaic, not-understood version of four centuries ago is inexcusable, and almost unconscionable.[2]

NOTES

1 For all practical purposes, there is virtually universal agreement that the Greek text underlying the King James is inferior. Although today a small handful of biblical professors hold that this text is to be preferred, most such professors reject it. The institutions where the latter

213

professors teach include Westminster, Dallas, Trinity Evangelical, Wheaton, Fuller, Bethel, Concordia, Gordon-Conwell, Southern Baptist, Southwestern Baptist, Wisconsin Lutheran, St Andrews, Covenant, Reformed, Western, Conservative Baptist, Nazarene, Princeton, Harvard, Yale, Goshen, Regent, Grace, Asbury, Western Evangelical, Reformed Episcopal, Cincinnati Bible, Wycliffe, Mennonite Brethren, Harding, Biblical and Luther Northwestern. The finest and most readable discussion of this problem is D. A. Carson's *The King James Version Debate* (Grand Rapids: Baker Book House, 1979).

2 Edwin H. Palmer, 'Dear Duncan: About that Review of the NIV . . .', *The Presbyterian Guardian* 44 (August–September 1975): 126–7.

SCRIPTURE INDEX

217

SCRIPTURE INDEX

SCRIPTURE INDEX

SCRIPTURE INDEX